"'He humbled himself': Jesus chose to 'make low'! Becoming humble is a verb! It is a choice we all can make, and I found Michele Howe's *The Humble Life*, a beautiful journey with Christ through the Gospels, as a wonderful way to better learn how and why walking in humility with Jesus is a healthier way to live."

—**Pam Farrel, co-director of Love-Wise and Proverbs 19:8 ministries, international speaker, and author of fifty-nine books**

"I enjoyed the twenty ways that Michele showed how walking a humble life requires submission to Jesus. Throughout the book, I enjoyed reading how Jesus' simple acts of obedience are our example to follow. It helped when she pointed to Jesus in the Scriptures and how she connected the heartfelt prayers at the end of each chapter and kept my focus more on my walk with Jesus and applying that prayer to seek him humbly."

—**Nancy Sabato, producer and host, *The Call with Nancy Sabato***

"Humility is transformative. A heart characterized by humility is approachable and safe. Author Michele Howe invites readers to exchange discontent, judgment, and striving of the self for the peaceful serenity of love rooted in life-giving humility. Following the powerful example of Jesus, we discover that in losing ourselves we find God is worthy of our trust."

—**PeggySue Wells, bestselling author of thirty-four books, including *Chasing Sunrise*, *The Patent*, and *The Ten Best Decisions a Single Mom Can Make***

THE HUMBLE LIFE

Books by Michele Howe from
Hendrickson Publishers

Burdens Do a Body Good:
Meeting Life's Challenges with Strength (and Soul)
(with Dr. Christopher A. Foetisch)

Caring for Your Aging Parents: Lessons
in Love, Loss, and Letting Go

Deliver Us: Finding Hope in the Psalms for Moments of Desperation

Empty Nest, What's Next? Parenting Adult
Children Without Losing Your Mind

Finding Freedom and Joy in Self-Forgetfulness

Giving Thanks for a Perfectly Imperfect Life

Going It Alone: Meeting the Challenges of Being a Single Mom

Grace & Gratitude for Everyday Life

The Humble Life: Walking with Jesus through the Gospels

Joyous Faith: The Key to Aging with Resilience

Navigating the Friendship Maze:
The Search for Authentic Friendship

Preparing, Adjusting, and Loving the Empty Nest
A companion to *Empty Nest, What's Next?*

Serving as Jesus Served: Practical Ways to Love Others

Still Going It Alone: Mothering with Faith and
Finesse When the Children Have Grown

Strength for All Seasons: A Prayer Devotional

There's a Reason They Call It GRANDparenting

THE HUMBLE LIFE

Walking with Jesus through the Gospels

MICHELE HOWE

an imprint of Hendrickson Publishing Group

The Humble Life: Walking with Jesus through the Gospels

© 2024 Michele Howe

Published by Hendrickson Publishers
an imprint of Hendrickson Publishing Group
Hendrickson Publishers, LLC
P. O. Box 3473
Peabody, Massachusetts 01961-3473
www.hendricksonpublishers.com

ISBN 978-1-4964-8529-8

Photo by Martino Pietropoli on Unsplash

Printed in the United States of America

First Printing — March 2024

Library of Congress Control Number: 2023946399

To my GRAND grands,

May each of you find the joy of humbly serving Jesus
as your Lord and Savior all the days of your lives.

Logan James Zatko
Tyler William Zatko
Jonathan Dale Zatko
Charis Myra Canning
Thea Eve Canning
Simon Anders Canning

Children's children are a crown to the aged.
Proverbs 17:6

Contents

Acknowledgments

As long as I can remember, I've loved books. I love reading books. I love perusing books in stores, online, and in libraries. The truth is, I love holding new books, old books—all kinds of books! I have found strength and solace in books during difficult times. I have been instructed and challenged by books that have been instrumental in my spiritual growth. I still remember the summer afternoon as a junior high school student sitting outside reading a magazine article written by a teenager and thinking to myself: *I could do this*! At that moment, I knew I wanted to be a writer. While that child's dream took many years to come to fruition, it did come.

After my first daughter was born in 1985, I began writing book reviews before moving on to articles, and finally in 1999, my first book was published by Hendrickson Publishers. Now, some twenty-four years later, I'm still writing for Hendrickson Publishers, and I'm both humbled and grateful to have the privilege of working with this amazingly talented team of publishing professionals. I love the longevity of working with the same fine publishing house season after season and year after year (and their exemplary staff makes it a joy).

Simply stated, I am one singularly blessed woman to enjoy the rare privilege of working together with the Hendrickson team. I've learned so much about the ins and outs of creating a book from each of these fine individuals whom I'm thrilled to name here so that you too can appreciate their priceless contributions to the book you now hold in your hands. My sincerest gratitude to the now-retired head of Hendrickson Publishers, Paul Hendrickson, who has been a tremendous encouragement throughout the years and consistently stood behind my writing ministry. Thank you, Paul! Let me say a giant-sized thank-you to Patricia Anders. As editorial director, you are a marvel at your job and a joy to work with. Thank you! Thanks also to production assistant, Nicole Viera, for your thoughtful and expert work on this book!

To Krista Squibb, marketing manager, I am always happy to see your name pop up in my inbox because you consistently encourage me with your kindness and your dedication to getting the word out on my books. Thank you to Phil Frank for his meticulous typesetting and to Dave Pietrantonio for getting my book to the printer and out to the world in record time. Thank you both! Finally, to Sarah Slattery for her beautiful cover design. Again and again, I love your work!

I also want to express my kindest appreciation to Bob Hostetler who represents me at the Steve Laube Agency. I appreciate you and your ongoing efforts on my behalf of my writing ministry.

And last, but most certainly not least, I want to offer my most heartfelt gratitude to my husband Jim of thirty-nine years who has always made sure I had room to write and the opportunity to do so. You've been my biggest supporter and behind the scenes prayer warrior—and do I ever know it! I love you, Honey.

 # Introduction

Therefore, as God's chosen people, holy and dearly loved, clothe yourselves with compassion, kindness, humility, gentleness and patience. Bear with each other and forgive one another if any of you has a grievance against someone. Forgive as the Lord forgave you. And over all these virtues put on love, which binds them all together in perfect unity.

Colossians 3:12–14

The Humble Life was birthed in my heart and mind when I began studying the topic of humility throughout Scripture. Each time I came across a new passage that discussed the key role that humility (as a godly character trait) played, I became increasingly drawn to this spiritual discipline. Contrasted with humility's opposite and unattractive trait, pride, I started noticing how powerfully God uses those who humble themselves before him. It was startling to me how frequently the Bible addresses a character quality so overlooked in our society and how essential developing it is to God in people's lives.

The more I delved into this theme of humility, the more I was convinced that my humility meter was far too low. Did I perceive myself as being prideful? No, I did not. What I did realize, however, was how far-reaching, how impactful it is to grow a humble heart that spills out through my words and deeds. As I studied the many passages in the Bible that paired humility with God's favor and blessings, I recognized the opposite warning as well.

> God opposes the proud but shows favor to the humble. (James 4:6)

> All of you, clothe yourselves with humility toward one another, because, "God opposes the proud but shows favor to the humble." Humble yourselves, therefore, under God's mighty hand, that he may lift you up in due time. (1 Pet. 5:5–6)

These passages tell us that God is indeed highly invested in growing us into humble men and women who image him well before an unbelieving world.

God also desires that we put the full weight of our trust in him despite the uncertainties we all face. He wants us to understand what a gift it is to us that he is reigning sovereignly over us—and that is a good thing. Only the humble in heart will view God's sovereignty as a blessing and be willing to lay aside their preferences, plans, and dreams to follow God's lead in their lives from a place of willing, joyful submission and humility. As God's beloved own children, we must learn to trust in his faithfulness, his goodness, and his abiding grace as we study Scripture in its entirety.

> The Son is the radiance of God's glory and the exact representation of his being, sustaining all things by his powerful word.
> (Heb. 1:3)

Since Jesus tells us that he is the full representation of the Father, what better way to fully understand God than to study how Jesus lived among his disciples and followers through the Gospels? In this book, you will walk alongside the disciples as they followed Jesus from town to town as we look at various

Gospel stories. You will learn how Jesus dealt with his followers (as well as those who opposed him) through a spirit of humility. His willingness to lay aside his divine rights as God's only Son to come to earth to live among us as a man is nothing but stunning when we contemplate his Godship. Jesus, by divine example, demonstrated through real-life experiences and powerful storytelling what living the humble life looks like—from the mundane to the magnificent.

As we read these marvelous and insightful accounts of Jesus as he taught and interacted with his disciples and followers, friends and family, strangers and enemies, we will notice a recurring theme: that of humility. Jesus was always in complete control of his emotions, and the way in which he lived and spoke to those around him offers us timeless wisdom and insight for our own daily lives. Are you ready to embark on this exciting adventure to discover how developing humility is a life-changer? Then let's get started!

Chapter 1

The Humble Understand That No Task Is Beneath Them

Jesus knew that the Father had put all things under his power, and that he had come from God and was returning to God; so he got up from the meal, took off his outer clothing, and wrapped a towel around his waist. After that, he poured water into a basin and began to wash his disciples' feet, drying them with the towel that was wrapped around him.

John 13:3–5

Jesus, always so observant of the internal conflicts brewing in the hearts of his disciples, took note of the situation surrounding him. He knew his time had come and that he was going to the Father. So, Jesus showed them the full extent of his love for them through his timely act of humble service. As he heard the disciples vying for positions of honor, he also knew that Judas was going to betray him. Silently, Jesus took measure of those around him and offered them a lesson on being a servant that they never forgot. He offered them a real-time example of what it means to lay aside one's rights as he took on the mantle of humble service shortly before he would lay his life down for each of them.

Jesus loved them well by seeing the glaring need—that of washing one another's feet—and so he quietly provided the disciples with an illustration of what it means to serve others in a way no one else would. Midway through the meal, Jesus stood and laid aside his garments, took a towel, and wrapped it around himself. Then he picked up a pitcher and into it began to pour the water, always symbolic of cleansing, following by his washing the disciples' dirty feet. We can assume they were taken aback by his actions; and although they would have been happy to wash Jesus' feet, none of them made a move to do this for their fellow disciples. Thus Jesus' powerful example of what it means to do a task of the lowest form (something a bond servant would normally do) started a domino effect of reactions from those in the room.

Thanks to John's writings, we know that when Jesus went to wash Peter's feet, Peter resisted as only Peter could by saying, "Lord, are you going to wash my feet?" Followed by another disclaimer from him, "No, you shall never wash my feet." To which Jesus answered, "Unless I wash you, you have no part with me." With his usual exuberance, Peter cried out, "Then, Lord, not just my feet but my hands and my head as well" (John 13:6–9). Peter may not have fully understood the eternal import of Jesus' words, but he wanted all that Jesus could offer even though he didn't fully grasp how he would be called to suffer for Christ in the years that would follow.

Jesus then asked his disciples if they understood what he had done by serving them. He underscored his lesson by saying,

> "You call me 'Teacher' and 'Lord,' and rightly so, for that is what I am. Now that I, your Lord and Teacher, have washed your feet, you also should wash one another's feet. I have set you an example

6

that you should do as I have done for you. Very truly I tell you, no servant is greater than his master, nor is a messenger greater than the one who sent him. Now that you know these things, you will be blessed if you do them." (John 13:13–17)

It's interesting to note that Jesus showed them the full extent of his love by choosing to humbly serve each of them.

We, too, must quietly contemplate the disciples' reactions to Jesus' act of service and his words of instruction. Jesus led by example. He humbled himself as the lowest servant and then issued that same command to his beloved disciples. Jesus' powerful yet quiet act of humility dramatically impacted everyone in that Upper Room. May it do the same for each of us today as we embrace every opportunity given to us to take on the mantle of humble service wherever we find it. And may we have the same holy desire to be thoroughly washed by Jesus' sacrifice on the cross so that we might serve in his stead as long as we have breath in our bodies.

※ ※ ※

Lowly and humble tasks—that's what (and where) most of us are called upon to put our hands and feet into action. When we're required to humble ourselves and serve in the lowest job conceivable to us, God wants us to remember his Son's example as he saw the need (that everyone else saw too) and met it. Without fanfare, without drawing undue attention to himself, Jesus simply rose and served without a word.

As I contemplate Jesus' example to us, I wonder how his disciples must have felt (and reacted) when they realized their Lord took on the lowest of tasks. Were they ashamed? Were they humbled? Probably. For my part, whenever I read this story, I'm certainly moved.

I believe one reason we often balk at having to take on unwanted jobs, tasks, and responsibilities is because we feel we're being unfairly imposed upon. Don't we sometimes inaccurately believe that we've paid our dues from past unsavory areas of service and that it's time for others to step up and do the dirty work for a while? But when we consider Jesus' powerful lesson as he quietly attended to the lowest acts of service in that day—washing filthy feet—we must reconsider (and retract) our former faulty attitudes toward lowly serving.

Most of our lives, we'll be faced with humble responsibilities that may feel beneath us. And that's okay. When we choose to relinquish our perceived rights and allow God to lead us wherever he deems best, everything changes. Our attitude shifts to one of obedience no matter what the cost to us personally. Our thinking realigns with what will count throughout eternity, not on our résumés. Our hearts are at peace, and we'll reflect the joy and gratitude of knowing that wherever Jesus places us, we're privileged to serve the king of all creation. If that single recognition isn't humbling enough, then we need to take a more introspective look into our hearts and ask ourselves if we truly understand what Paul in Romans 12:1 encourages us to do. "Offer your bodies as a living sacrifice, holy and pleasing to God—this is your true and proper worship." Day by day, in lowly acts of service, we honor Jesus when we're ready to serve with our hands and hearts.

My Heart's Cry to You, O Lord

Father, thank you for reminding me of Jesus' humble example that no act of service is beneath me. Help me to view every opportunity to love and serve others as the divine privilege it is. Give me wisdom and insight so that I recognize that my life belongs to you. May I find joy in selfless service no matter what form it takes. Clothe me with humility, Lord. Clothe me with a spirit of holy gratitude. Make me an instrument of love, joy, and peace so that the world can see how great your love for it is. Amen.

The Humble Life in Everyday Life

1. **Humility before God.** *Jesus knew that the Father had put all things under his power, and that he had come from God and was returning to God.* Remind yourself of Jesus' example as he focused on the eternal not the temporal. Jesus wants you to keep your eyes on what matters most in eternity and not get sidetracked by the world's definition of success and service.

2. **Humility before others.** *Jesus poured water into a basin and began to wash his disciples' feet.* This week, purpose to serve others without complaint, without objection. Endeavor to bless, encourage, and bring eternal hope to those with whom you come into contact.

3. **Humility of heart.** *Jesus got up from the meal, took off his outer clothing, and wrapped a towel around his waist.* Pray that God will create in you a humble, compassionate, and merciful heart compelled to love, serve, and care for the needs of those around you.

Chapter 2

Humble Everyday Service Reveals Our Hearts

"Then the righteous will answer him, 'Lord, when did we see you hungry and feed you, or thirsty and give you something to drink? When did we see you a stranger and invite you in, or needing clothes and clothe you? When did we see you sick or in prison and go to visit you?'

"The King will reply, 'Truly I tell you, whatever you did for one of the least of these brothers and sisters of mine, you did for me.'"

Matthew 25:37–40

Jesus crafted his lessons to his disciples in utterly practical and eternally significant ways. He spoke with them in veiled parables, too, yes. But often he offered them everyday life scenarios from which to better understand the point he wanted them to grasp. Jesus describes the difference between sheep and goats in the verses above from the Gospel of Matthew. Specifically, he delineates the difference between those who will share in his inheritance as opposed to those who will not. Jesus then continues to describe how the attitudes of our hearts (in

11

life and in humble service) give way to the outer recognition of whether or not we belong to him.

Here in Matthew 25, Jesus is helping to clarify what it looks like to be a servant and a disciple. He gives them concrete examples of what it means to demonstrate to others practical, loving service in his name. The righteous reveal their regenerated hearts by their willingness to offer hospitality in its most meager form. A cup of water. A meal. A piece of clothing. A visit to the sick. A conversation to encourage someone in prison. Jesus wanted his beloved disciples to understand the blessing of service offered in his name in everyday situations. He wanted them to open their eyes to opportunities that are actually divine opportunities that reveal they belong to him. In this passage, Jesus contrasts the difference between sheep (his followers) and goats (those of unbelief), and he does so by illustrating that our outer acts of service reveal the spiritual condition of our hearts.

Beyond this life lesson, Jesus wants to impart to his listeners is the deeper truth of the coming judgment and how he would separate the sheep from the goats. Explaining this to them in a way they would understand, Jesus uses simple opportunities to highlight the condition of their hearts. Jesus wants his disciples to hear and understand first and foremost that each of them needs to acknowledge him as their Lord and Savior. Only then could he begin to broaden how their walk of faith as seen through the definition of service—that whatever we do for "the least of these" defines our heart's attitude. We are to see Christ in everyone we meet, to love them as we would love him if he had such a need. Jesus didn't make his command lofty, obscure, or confusing. No, he brought the immensity of the divine challenge down to the barest of human levels. Recognize the condition of your heart first. See a need. Then meet the need.

Apparently, his listeners required such simplicity, as do we. They needed Jesus—the "King" in the parable—to play it straight with them by first dealing with their heart condition. Did they belong to him or not? If they call themselves followers of Christ, then they needed to demonstrate this living faith by meeting the needs of those around them. Jesus details several practical ways to serve him by serving others. We can wonder at their response. Did they have an aha moment? Did they expect something completely different from the Lord? Something grander and more ostentatious? We really don't know the answers to these questions from this passage. But we might guess at some of the answers by how we respond when we read Jesus' words today. First, be sure you know Jesus as Savior and Lord. And then see to it that your life and your acts of service are in sync with your relationship with Christ. Our faith and our actions should express themselves in complementary ways. If our hearts belong to Jesus, then our actions should reflect that love toward others that will work itself out through meeting the needs of those around us, however humbling on our part.

※ ※ ※

This simple everyday service principle (and practice), however, goes further than just seeing a need and meeting it. How so? Jesus wants his disciples to understand that once they accepted him as Lord and Savior, their everyday service toward others would reflect that reborn inner heart condition.

Jesus already knew the condition of their hearts (as he knows ours), and he recognized the disciples had layers of social conditioning to overcome. He knew how they felt about those they came into contact with who were different from themselves. He knew they would struggle against serving anyone they deemed as an enemy or "unclean." And yet, Jesus says, "Truly I tell you, whatever you did for one of the least of these brothers and sisters of mine, you did for me." Because you belong to me, Jesus says, go and humbly serve the least of these.

How can we begin to serve those we deem as "the least of these"? Who in your life do you bristle against helping? Do you even know the needs of those around you? Let's not confine Jesus' definition of the "least of these" to the materially poor or downtrodden. There are people with needs everywhere we look—from those who simply need a listening ear to even just receiving a warm smile. It could be your letter carrier or someone at work or church.

And then there are those with much deeper needs you find hard to deal with. Do you balk at having yet another difficult conversation with that person who never seems to listen or take advice? Have you given up on someone who has stumbled so many times, you feel hopeless they will ever change? Do you get impatient when a brother or sister seems to demand assistance rather than ask with a sense of gratitude or common courtesy? Do you protect yourself (your time, energy, or material resources) from those who might ask too much of you?

We need to remember that Jesus didn't tell his disciples to go out and meet *every* need. Clearly, he was aiming at the attitude of their hearts. He wanted them to be alert and sensitive to the possibilities they would come across in their daily lives. He wanted them to serve others as they would serve him. Jesus desires the same of his followers today. We must have hearts in tune with the Holy Spirit and be sensitive to God's nudges to willingly walk into a situation with simple obedience. May each of us heed his words, answer this call, and seek to humbly serve those around us. We must remind ourselves that our faith and our actions should express themselves in complementary ways. If our hearts belong to Jesus, then our actions should reflect that love toward others.

My Heart's Cry to You, O Lord

Father, thank you for Jesus' simple way of teaching his disciples how to serve everyone. Help me to be alert and sensitive to the needs of those you bring before me. Help me to have a heart willing to sacrifice all I have, all I am, for the sake of those I'm able to help. Give me a heart that never puts limits on my service. Give me discernment and wisdom to know how and whom to serve. Show me the most loving way to easing the suffering of those around me. And may I always serve in Jesus' name. Amen.

The Humble Life in Everyday Life

1. **Humility before God.** *"Truly I tell you, whatever you did for one of the least of these brothers and sisters of mine, you did for me."* Ask God to create in you a pure heart that desires to serve others out of your great love for him. Be mindful of your own neediness before God and how much you rely on his faithful goodness every single day of your life.

2. **Humility before others.** *"Truly I tell you, whatever you did for one of the least of these brothers and sisters of mine, you did for me."* This week, be aware of any tendencies you may have to think more highly of yourself than you should. Be sensitive to any critical or judgmental attitudes you may be harboring in your heart.

3. **Humility of heart.** *"Truly I tell you, whatever you did for one of the least of these brothers and sisters of mine, you did for me."* Pray for divine opportunities to demonstrate the love of Christ to others in practical ways as you move through your day. Be ready to lend a hand or supply a need as the Lord directs you in whatever form that service may take.

Chapter 3

The Humble Judge Their Own Hearts Accurately

"Do not judge, or you too will be judged. For in the same way you judge others, you will be judged, and with the measure you use, it will be measured to you.

"Why do you look at the speck of sawdust in your brother's eye and pay no attention to the plank in your own eye? How can you say to your brother, 'Let me take the speck out of your eye,' when all the time there is a plank in your own eye? You hypocrite, first take the plank out of your own eye, and then you will see clearly to remove the speck from your brother's eye."

Matthew 7:1–5

If there was any passage of Scripture that instantly captures believers' attention, it's this message from Jesus on judging others. I mean, who among us hasn't passed judgment on someone else? In this chapter in Matthew's Gospel, Jesus continues his Sermon on the Mount (which began in Matthew 5), speaking about the dangers of passing judgment on others before he launches into instructions on prayer, recognizing true and false prophets and disciples, and then closing out with the parable of the wise and foolish builders. Throughout this chapter, Jesus illustrates that there's a wise versus a foolish path to take.

In the opening paragraph, we hear Jesus warn his disciples and all those listening to him about rendering judgment on others. Since we too are sinners, how can we pass judgment on another person? Jesus makes his point clear, "Do not judge, or you too will be judged. For in the same way you judge others, you will be judged, and with the measure you use, it will be measured to you." He's warning his listeners not to be critical of others, to the point of calling them hypocrites. He calls for them—and us—to consider their (and our) own weaknesses, struggles, and sins. Remember and consider, Jesus says, your sins first and foremost. Remember that in the same measure you judge others, God will judge you. This is serious stuff. Jesus speaks directly to his disciples about their inclination (and ours) to see themselves as more righteous than others.

He then elaborates by asking, "Why do you look at the speck of sawdust in your brother's eye and pay no attention to the plank in your own eye?" As he presses further into the heart of the matter, he compels us to understand a pivotal issue within our own hearts that needs to be addressed. Here, Jesus gave his disciples the gift of exaggerated hyperbole by contrasting the obvious sin of a tiny splinter we may see in another person as opposed to the gigantic plank in our own eye. How can we rightly pass judgment on another's "splinter," when we're essentially blinded by our own "plank"? The truth is we cannot. We dare not.

Thus Jesus tells his disciples to stop this kind of judgment in its tracks. Take an honest, introspective look into your own heart and life, and then prayerfully confess your sin to God. Heart motives matter. He is calling every individual who calls themselves a Christ-follower to look at the condition of their own heart and stop getting sidetracked by passing judgment on others as a method of deflecting, minimizing, or condoning our own sin.

✳ ✳ ✳

It's so easy to observe the failings and mistakes in others' lives and mentally pass a silent verdict on them. It takes much less effort to do this rather than look deeper into the issues of our own hearts that may be causing us to fall and fail. Jesus is warning us that judgment begins in the heart. My task, my responsibility, is to take a long, hard introspective look into the condition of my own heart. My job isn't to jump headlong into passing judgment on the person I've silently convicted to make my own sin seem less heinous.

As Jesus taught, we must stop and look at ourselves and get in right standing with God through personal confession and prayer. Only then will we be able to view others through the lens of God's boundless grace and forgiveness. Only when we recognize our sin in its true and destructive form and receive God's forgiveness can we see others' weaknesses and failings in a compassionate light. As we learn to stand before the Lord in honest transparency and seek his pardon for every sin great and small can we then break the destructive habit of being judgmental. Jesus could not have made his point clearer here: "Do not judge, or you too will be judged." This statement with all its repercussions should serve as both a stern warning and a kind admonition from our merciful Savior who forgave us when we were still his enemies.

My Heart's Cry to You, O Lord

Father, I need to confess my heart attitudes to you. I've been sinfully focusing on the faults and failings of others around me. I've neglected to look deeply into my own heart and identify where I'm faltering. Please forgive me for my sinful heart that too often easily points out the failings of others but doesn't recognize my own personal sin. Help me to keep my accounts clear with you as my highest priority. Help me to keep my eyes on you, Lord, and clothe me with a humble, compassionate, gentle spirit that reflects your perfect love for your children. Amen.

The Humble Life in Everyday Life

1. **Humility before God.** *"Do not judge, or you too will be judged."* Spend time each day this week asking the Lord to reveal your sinful heart attitudes. As God shows you areas of sinfulness, confess and ask for forgiveness and then be humbly grateful for his ongoing faithful love toward you.

2. **Humility before others.** *"For in the same way you judge others, you will be judged, and with the measure you use, it will be measured to you."* Ask the Lord to show you where you've been judgmental toward others. Pray for those you have judged and ask God to show them mercy, bring hope and healing, and do a great work of spiritual restoration as needed in both of your lives.

3. **Humility of heart.** *"You hypocrite, first take the plank out of your own eye, and then you will see clearly to remove the speck from your brother's eye."* Write down what God has been showing you about your own struggles with sinful judging. Locate several Bible verses that help you stay on the path and then write them down in your journal.

 # Chapter 4

The Godward Heart Speaks with Humility

*"No good tree bears bad fruit, nor does a bad tree bear
good fruit. Each tree is recognized by its own fruit. People
do not pick figs from thornbushes, or grapes from briers.
A good man brings good things out of the good stored
up in his heart, and an evil man brings evil things out
of the evil stored up in his heart. For the mouth speaks
what the heart is full of."*

Luke 6:43–45

In this passage, Jesus presents his stunning yet practical
lesson on trees and their accompanying fruit. Here we see
him comparing the difference between a good tree and a
bad tree as it pertains to the types of fruit each produces. Jesus'
logical conclusion is that the root of a tree is synonymous with
one's heart condition and the fruit we bear will reflect either a
heart submitted to God or not. Jesus colorfully explains to his
disciples the truth of this principle by sharing various analo-
gies with them from the natural created world. "No good tree
bears bad fruit, nor does a bad tree bear good fruit. Each tree is
recognized by its own fruit." Jesus says it plainly. Good tree.
Good fruit. Bad tree. Bad fruit.

He continues by emphasizing the commonsense truth, "People do not pick figs from thornbushes, or grapes from briers." As men and women of that day who were well acquainted with the agricultural world, they would have likely been nodding in agreement as Jesus underscored this obvious point: Good doesn't come from evil nor does evil produce good. This principle is the precursor to the main truth he wants to make. "A good man brings good things out of the good stored up in his heart, and an evil man brings evil things out of the evil stored up in his heart." It's either one or the other. Not both. Jesus tells his disciples that if their hearts are submitted to God, then the outpouring of their hearts will result in good fruit—the kind of "fruit" that naturally pours from lives characterized by service, selflessness, and unconditional love. Add to this outward evidence of a transformed heart by what we say: "For the mouth speaks what the heart is full of."

Again, Jesus plainly tells us that if God has transformed our hearts, then our good fruit will reflect that inner holiness. If, on the other hand, our hearts are still bound in sin, then our fruit can only be bad. His point? It's all about the condition of our hearts. What erupts from our lives (by way of our words and deeds) will tell one and all who our hearts and souls belong to. Jesus doesn't offer any middle ground here. It's an either/or proposition. As in all his teachings, Jesus demands those who call him Lord to abandon everything else to follow him with all their heart.

※ ※ ※

Perhaps the most difficult part of this lesson to acknowledge is that the condition of our heart is apparent for everyone to see. Ouch. Jesus made it abundantly clear in his message to his followers that a good person will bring forth good fruit whereas an evil person will bring forth evil. Again, Jesus doesn't allow any middle ground for his followers then or now. This principle holds true for us today.

Jesus is issuing a warning to be introspective and circumspect about the condition of our hearts. As those who call ourselves followers of Jesus, we need to consider if the outward evidence that springs forth from our lives reflects a transformed and redeemed individual or not? Do your day-to-day choices, acts of service, and speech rightly reflect a heart that has been forgiven through the cleansing blood of Christ and made righteous? Is the fruit of your life overflowing with humility, mercy, and compassion?

In other words, when others look at your life and mine, do they see a reflection of our Lord and Savior? Or do they observe the opposite of what we say we live for and believe? For most of us, I would guess we wouldn't have to look very far back to identify streaks of selfishness, irritability, and even unkindness. Our choices might indeed sinfully reflect our stubborn willfulness as we pursue goals that are solely self-serving. Our words of choice might reflect a hardened, prideful heart that criticizes others.

Again, none of us can hide the true condition of our hearts. When we get our own way, it is, of course, much easier to exhibit a lovingly humble and kind demeanor. But when we're opposed, inconvenienced, or wronged, it's then that the test of our hearts' true master will be visible to all. Jesus' message is a timely one. If only each of us would take time today to humbly and prayerfully reflect on our past week and the various difficulties and impasses we encountered. For those who observed our actions and heard our words, would they characterize us as bearing good fruit or evil? Would they wonder who our master truly is?

My Heart's Cry to You, O Lord

Father, Jesus' lesson on the trees that bear good or evil fruit hits home to me. I'm convinced that if the attitude of my heart was visible to the world, it wouldn't reflect your unconditional love toward others. I'm ashamed of how I have spoken in moments of anger and frustration. Help me, Lord, to turn my heart back toward you and to humble myself so that my heart is rightly submissive to your plan for me. Give me your wisdom and understanding during difficult times. Help me to rightly reflect your perfect love to others even when life is especially painful or distressing. I long to bear the good fruit you talk about. Please continue to do your sanctifying work within me. Amen.

The Humble Life in Everyday Life

1. **Humility before God.** *"No good tree bears bad fruit, nor does a bad tree bear good fruit. Each tree is recognized by its own fruit."* This week, prayerfully spend time before God asking him to reveal any wayward or sinful heart attitudes that need to be confessed and forsaken. Humbly reflect upon the past week and your interactions with others by asking God to show you what kind of fruit your heart and life are producing.

2. **Humility before others.** *"For the mouth speaks what the heart is full of."* Spend time thinking about recent conversations you've had. Were these exchanges characterized by a humble heart and compassionate speech? If not, initiate a conversation with those you may have offended to ask for their forgiveness.

3. **Humility of heart.** *"A good man brings good things out of the good stored up in his heart, and an evil man brings evil things out of the evil stored up in his heart."* Pray for God to reveal any pride within your heart. Ask him to create in you a heart sensitive to sin and a desire for holiness in both attitude and action.

Chapter 5

The Humble Love Others More Than Themselves

"My command is this: Love each other as I have loved you. Greater love has no one than this: to lay down one's life for one's friends. You are my friends if you do what I command. I no longer call you servants, because a servant does not know his master's business. Instead, I have called you friends, for everything that I learned from my Father I have made known to you. You did not choose me, but I chose you and appointed you so that you might go and bear fruit—fruit that will last—and so that whatever you ask in my name the Father will give you. This is my command: Love each other."

John 15:12–17

I appreciate how the Gospel of John opens with Jesus' parable of the vine and the branches: "I am the true vine, and my Father is the gardener." Jesus explains to his disciples that for them to become fruitful, God will have to prune the sin (and immaturity) from their lives so that they will be productive as they grow in godliness. Jesus says that they must learn to abide in him. As they remain in Jesus and his words remain in them, they will naturally obey his commands.

This leads to Jesus teaching his disciples, "Love each other as I have loved you. Greater love has no one than this: to lay down one's life for one's friends." Once again, Jesus gently sets the stage for the disciples to mesh the principles of choosing to follow him with the moment-by-moment decisions that reflect that choice. He wants them to connect the dots between a continual abiding with him and their ability to fulfill this lofty command. Jesus knows that unless they remain in him and his words dwell within their hearts, they cannot obey this challenging edict.

He continues by telling them that they are not mere servants who don't know their master's business. Rather, he has granted them the elevated status of true friends—friends who not only walk alongside Jesus but also obey their Lord's commands. Jesus assures them of this special position because he has made known to them everything he has learned from the Father. As if being friends with Jesus isn't enough, he says, "You did not choose me, but I chose you and appointed you so that you might go and bear fruit—fruit that will last."

If the disciples ever doubted their beloved position with Christ before, this statement leaves them fully assured. And yet, Jesus speaks directly to the challenge of loving others as he does—of being willing to lay down one's life for another. The interchange that Jesus describes between abiding closely with the Father is important. If we are to be equipped to serve others in the ultimate extreme then we need to stay in close communion with Christ (his words must dwell within our hearts). Otherwise we cannot expect to fulfill Jesus' high command to love others as he has loved us. In ourselves, we're not able (nor desirous) to think more of others than ourselves. It's only through the supernatural abiding in the Holy Spirit's work in us that enables us to obey Jesus' commands to lay down our lives for others.

✳ ✳ ✳

Christ teaches us two important lessons here. First, as branches on the vine, we are utterly dependent on God as the gardener who sustains us, cares for us, prunes us, and makes us fruitful. As Jesus says, "You did not choose me, but I chose you and appointed you so that you might go and bear fruit—fruit that will last." God chose us. God appointed us. God commands us to bear fruit in his name that will last.

Second, it's only through this intimate abiding in him that we are equipped and able to fulfill his command: "Love each other as I have loved you. Greater love has no one than this: to lay down one's life for one's friends." With God as our expert gardener, we will bear fruit that will last. As long as our master gardener carefully tends to the needs of the vine as it grows and matures, we will always thrive under the capable and loving hand of the one who knows how to prune us so that we grow into fruitful individuals. As God nurtures us through his guiding hands, we must humbly choose to place ourselves fully into his care and keeping. The picture here is one of complete trust and utter dependence.

As we place ourselves entirely under God's care and submit to his plans for our lives, we will produce fruit that will stand the test of time. Only when we humbly submit ourselves to his pruning will we be ready to fulfill his command to place others' welfare above our own. As we abide in him, as we are changed by him, only then can we selflessly, humbly love others first and foremost. It's this two-pronged truth of abiding and submitting to God's pruning that enables us to fulfill his command to love each other as he has loved us.

My Heart's Cry to You, O Lord

Father, please help me to understand what it means to abide in you day by day. Give me your divine wisdom to humbly, willingly, even joyfully submit to your pruning in my life. I know that my heart isn't always prepared to lay my life down for others in love. Teach me that I'm only equipped to fulfill your commandment to love others as you loved me when I willingly submit myself to your instruction and corrective discipline. Thank you for choosing and appointing me so that I can go and bear fruit in your name—fruit that will last for all eternity. Amen.

The Humble Life in Everyday Life

1. **Humility before God.** *"You did not choose me, but I chose you and appointed you so that you might go and bear fruit—fruit that will last."* Take a few minutes each day to look up Bible passages that define fruit that lasts, such as Galatians 5:22 where Paul speaks of the fruit of the Spirit. Commit this verse to memory this week as a reminder of what spiritual fruit looks like in a real-world sense.

2. **Humility before others.** *"This is my command: Love each other."* Spend time praying for those closest to you this week while asking the Lord to reveal to you the ways you can encourage and support these individuals. Find ways to show them you love them through a spirit of humility and grace.

3. **Humility of heart.** *"Love each other as I have loved you. Greater love has no one than this: to lay down one's*

life for one's friends." Pray that God will create in you a selfless, humble heart that always seeks the best for others even when that "best" may inconvenience you. Look for practical ways to demonstrate this magnificent love for others each day this week.

Chapter 6

The Humble Are Willing to Forgive

Then Peter came to Jesus and asked, "Lord, how many times shall I forgive my brother or sister who sins against me? Up to seven times?"

Jesus answered, "I tell you, not seven times, but seventy-seven times.

"Therefore, the kingdom of heaven is like a king who wanted to settle accounts with his servants. As he began the settlement, a man who owed him ten thousand bags of gold was brought to him. Since he was not able to pay, the master ordered that he and his wife and his children and all that he had be sold to repay the debt.

"At this the servant fell on his knees before him. 'Be patient with me,' he begged, 'and I will pay back everything.' The servant's master took pity on him, canceled the debt and let him go.

"But when that servant went out, he found one of his fellow servants who owed him a hundred silver coins. He grabbed him and began to choke him. 'Pay back what you owe me!' he demanded.

"His fellow servant fell to his knees and begged him, 'Be patient with me, and I will pay it back.'

"But he refused. Instead, he went off and had the man thrown into prison until he could pay the debt. When the other servants saw what had happened, they were outraged and went and told their master everything that had happened.

"Then the master called the servant in. 'You wicked servant,' he said, 'I canceled all that debt of yours because you begged me to. Shouldn't you have had mercy on your fellow servant just as I had on you?' In anger his master handed him over to the jailers to be tortured, until he should pay back all he owed.

"This is how my heavenly Father will treat each of you unless you forgive your brother or sister from your heart."

Matthew 18:21–35

When Peter asks Jesus for clarification on how many times he should forgive offenses by others, Jesus doesn't respond as Peter had hoped. He thought that he would be doing well if he could forgive someone up to seven times. Jesus clearly is trying to teach his disciples that the question is not how many times they ought to forgive, but how it is with the attitude of their hearts. In fact, Jesus very well might have said to Peter, "Why are you even asking me this question after you have been forgiven all your sins by your heavenly Father?" But Jesus didn't. Instead, he offered Peter a parable none of them would ever forget.

He began setting the stage by telling Peter that it's not enough to follow the law and forgive up to seven times; they are to forgive an unlimited number of times. Go beyond the prescribed law, far beyond, Jesus tells them—even to the point of relinquishing all your grievances (and debts owed to you by others) before the throne of God. Jesus, the master storyteller, then tells the tale of two servants who owed money, focusing on their responses and what it revealed about them.

The first servant owed his master an amount so great it would have been impossible to repay in his lifetime. The master had every right to place him, his wife, and children in prison as partial repayment. But when the servant begged for mercy and forgiveness, the master graciously gave it. What then did this forgiven servant do? Instead of offering the same measure of forgiveness to his fellow servant who owed him less than three months' wages, he condemned him and put him in prison. He showed no mercy although he himself had been the beneficiary of the master's extravagant forgiveness.

Here, Jesus allows the weight of this scenario to take root in the disciples' hearts and minds. He wants them to consider how unjustly the servant acted after being forgiven himself. Then he explains the master's rightful anger at the unforgiving servant's actions by calling him wicked and handing him over to the jailers. Jesus' point? Stop and consider what God has done when he forgave all your sins and made you heirs to the kingdom of heaven. Stop and consider the heavy weight God has lifted from your shoulders and how he offered mercy in its place. Stop and consider this debt of grace you now owe God from this moment forward before you refuse to forgive and withhold mercy from others. Stop and consider that God will treat you as the master treated his ungrateful servant if you refuse to forgive. God won't withdraw his redemptive forgiveness (eternal salvation) from his beloved children; but when we disobey by refusing to forgive others, we can't enjoy the intimacy and peace with our heavenly Father until we confess and forgive. By not offering forgiveness to others, we forfeit this precious fellowship with God that should be our highest priority far and above clinging to a grievance we have against someone.

✳ ✳ ✳

In this passage, we see how easily we might fall into the same trap as the disciples when Peter asked about the limits of offering forgiveness. I wonder how many of us have been on the receiving end of another's sinful actions and struggled to forgive that person. We may rightfully feel grieved, disappointed, or injured. Yet, Jesus still issues us the same command that he gave to Peter and the disciples. Forgive seventy-times seven. In other words, don't count the number of times you're required to forgive others. Simply forgive.

We all know, however, that it sounds much easier to say we'll forgive than to actually do so. First, let's clarify what forgiveness is and what it isn't. Forgiveness is a decision we make to let go of an offense and not bring it up again later. Forgiveness is a deliberate choice we make as the Holy Spirit enables us to do it. Forgiveness means we give over any thoughts of retribution or revenge to God and let God be the judge in place of us.

Forgiveness isn't necessarily trusting the person who sinned against you. Forgiveness is not placing yourself in a similar situation where another can hurt you. Forgiveness isn't a feeling nor is it necessarily forgetting what occurred. Forgiveness is a commitment to continue to forgive when painful memories of the offense surface again. All that said, Jesus tells us to forgive our offenders as God has forgiven us.

Jesus wants us to contemplate the greater truth here, which is that each of us has been pardoned by God for every one of our sins. Jesus paid the ultimate price for us when he suffered and died on the cross in place of us. When we meditate on this amazing gift of salvation and eternal life, it leaves us no excuse for harboring a spirit of unforgiveness toward others in this temporal world.

My Heart's Cry to You, O Lord

Father, I confess that I'm often not swift to forgive someone when they offend me. I dwell too long on the hurt and the sin instead of running to you with my heartache. Please help me to remember the great sacrifice Jesus paid in my place. Never let me forget that you have forgiven every one of my sins and that I'm now secure in your love for all eternity. Surely, as I reflect on this wonderful costly gift of forgiveness and grace, I can humbly forgive others fully and freely. Amen.

The Humble Life in Everyday Life

1. **Humility before God.** *"Then the master called the servant in. 'You wicked servant,' he said, 'I canceled all that debt of yours because you begged me to. Shouldn't you have had mercy on your fellow servant just as I had on you?'"* Today, spend time in prayer asking God to reveal to you any present grievances you're holding against others. Purpose to forgive each offense and allow the Lord to be the rightful judge over the situation.

2. **Humility before others.** *"Lord, how many times shall I forgive my brother or sister who sins against me? Up to seven times?" Jesus answered, "I tell you, not seven times, but seventy-seven times."* Each evening this week, take time to prayerfully reflect on conversations with others and review any sinful attitudes you may be harboring against someone. Prayerfully choose to first forgive and then pray for your offender every day.

3. **Humility of heart.** *"In anger the master handed him over to the jailers to be tortured, until he should pay back all he owed. This is how my heavenly Father will treat each of you unless you forgive your brother or sister from*

your heart." Focus each day on God's great gift of salvation and forgiveness of sins through Jesus on your behalf. Remind yourself that Jesus paid the ultimate price and that any sin against you by another pales in comparison.

Chapter 7

Humility Looks Good on Everyone

Then the mother of Zebedee's sons came to Jesus with her sons and, kneeling down, asked a favor of him.

"What is it you want?" he asked.

She said, "Grant that one of these two sons of mine may sit at your right and the other at your left in your kingdom."

"You don't know what you are asking," Jesus said to them. "Can you drink the cup I am going to drink?"

"We can," they answered.

Jesus said to them, "You will indeed drink from my cup, but to sit at my right or left is not for me to grant. These places belong to those for whom they have been prepared by my Father."

When the ten heard about this, they were indignant with the two brothers. Jesus called them together and said, "You know that the rulers of the Gentiles lord it over them, and their high officials exercise authority over them. Not so with you. Instead, whoever wants to become great among you must be your servant, and whoever wants to be first must be your slave—just as the Son of Man did not come to be served, but to serve, and to give his life as a ransom for many."

Matthew 20:20–28

In the NIV version I'm using for this text, the title for this section reads, "A Mother's Request," which I found both interesting and instructive. James and John's mother asked Jesus if he would promise to give her two sons the most prominent places next to him in the coming kingdom. Jesus gently responds to her (and them) by saying, "You don't know what you are asking." He continues by posing this direct question to the brothers to help them understand the weightiness of her audacious request. "Can you drink the cup I am going to drink?" Without missing a beat or taking the time to consider Jesus' words, they answer him, "We can."

He then tells of their future fate: "You will indeed drink from my cup, but to sit at my right or left is not for me to grant. These places belong to those for whom they have been prepared by my Father." Here Jesus refers to drinking from "my cup" as it relates to the suffering he will endure at the cross. Both James and John will follow him in their own suffering. We may wonder if Jesus was chastising James and John finally for assuming they would be worthy of these two privileged seats of honor in the kingdom. Did their mother finally understand the import of what she had asked and how inappropriate it was?

The remaining ten disciples were likewise not happy with James and John, and from their mutually angry response, we learn about the position of their hearts as well. If their hearts were rightfully humble, then it wouldn't have mattered what request James and John's mother had for her sons. But here we read that they all responded with indignation. Telling, isn't it? So, Jesus must not only address the heart attitudes of James, John, and their mother but the ten other disciples as well.

The lesson continues as Jesus points out to them how the rulers of the Gentiles lord themselves over everyone. Then he says, "Not so with you. Instead, whoever wants to become great among you must be your servant, and whoever wants to be first must be your slave—just as the Son of Man did not come to be served, but to serve, and to give his life as a ransom for many." Did the two brothers, their mother, and the other disciples get the message? Maybe. But hopefully, we do. Of course, we have the advantage of unpacking it from a historical distance. Once again, we watch how Jesus takes the measure of the disciples' hearts and reveals it to them using everyday-life scenarios. Jesus could very well have said, "Humility looks good on everyone."

※ ※ ※

As we study this passage of Scripture, our initial response might be one of incredulity. Each time I read this story, I'm amazed that James and John's mother had the boldness to ask Jesus to place her sons in the most prominent positions in the coming kingdom. Didn't she know how presumptuous she sounded? Didn't she stop to think about how the other ten disciples might respond? She doesn't seem to be in tune with Jesus' ongoing message (and perfect example) of selflessness and humility. It's stunning to me that she was internally unaware of her own heart motives.

Yet, how often do we see something we want (for ourselves or our families) and press forward with requests in a similar fashion? It's my hope that as Christ-followers, we would check our own desires to see if they're actually sinful and use the self-control given us by the Holy Spirit to rein in any such selfishness. But in the day to day, we can all admit to failing in this area of becoming a servant to others. Our desires must be sifted through the lens of our hearts as seen through the humility of our own Lord. As Jesus taught his disciples, we must ask ourselves the same question. If we also want to be his disciples, then we'll willingly and humbly choose to become servant and slave to all.

My Heart's Cry to You, O Lord

Father, help me to know the true condition of my heart. Am I seeking to become a humble, selfless servant, a servant to all? Or am I cherishing prideful desires, seeking the best for myself over the welfare of others? Give me the wisdom and insight I need to look honestly within my heart and confess any sins I may be nurturing. I want to grow into a disciple who reflects Jesus' consistently service-minded attitude. Please hear my prayer and continue your precious work of sanctification within my heart and mind. Amen.

The Humble Life in Everyday Life

1. **Humility before God.** *"Whoever wants to become great among you must be your servant, and whoever wants to be first must be your slave—just as the Son of Man did not come to be served, but to serve, and to give his life as a ransom for many."* Spend time each evening this week reviewing the day and being mindful of any heart attitudes that reveal inwardly (or outwardly) prideful and selfish desires. Ask God to create in you a pure heart that delights in serving him in whatever capacity he chooses to place you.

2. **Humility before others.** *"Whoever wants to become great among you must be your servant, and whoever wants to be first must be your slave—just as the Son of Man did not come to be served, but to serve, and to give his life as a ransom for many."* Focus this week on looking for practical ways to serve others. Ask God to show you creative ways to make a positive difference in the lives of others by looking out for their interests above your own.

3. **Humility of heart.** *"Whoever wants to become great among you must be your servant, and whoever wants to be first must be your slave—just as the Son of Man did not come to be served, but to serve, and to give his life as a ransom for many."* Prayerfully take a few moments each day to journal the thoughts and feelings you experienced this week that forced you to confront any pride or selfishness. Ask God to clothe you with a spirit of humility and grace that will cover a multitude of sins, including a heart that wrestles with selfishness and pride.

Chapter 8

The Humble Rely on God's Help
to Battle Temptation

Then Jesus went with his disciples to a place called Gethsemane, and he said to them, "Sit here while I go over there and pray." He took Peter and the two sons of Zebedee along with him, and he began to be sorrowful and troubled. Then he said to them, "My soul is over-whelmed with sorrow to the point of death. Stay here and keep watch with me."

Going a little farther, he fell with his face to the ground and prayed, "My Father, if it is possible, may this cup be taken from me. Yet not as I will, but as you will."

Then he returned to his disciples and found them sleeping. "Couldn't you men keep watch with me for one hour?" he asked Peter. "Watch and pray so that you will not fall into temptation. The spirit is willing, but the flesh is weak."

He went away a second time and prayed, "My Father, if it is not possible for this cup to be taken away unless I drink it, may your will be done."

Matthew 26:36–42

Thishis chapter of Matthew's Gospel is fraught with highly charged emotional scenes that crescendo just prior to the conversations Jesus has with his beloved disciples in the Garden of Gethsemane. Note that in the hours before this fateful evening, Jesus tells his disciples of the upcoming plot to kill him, Mary anoints Jesus with her alabaster flask of oil, Jesus and his disciples take part in the Passover meal where he announces that one of the Twelve will betray him, and finally, Jesus predicts Peter's subsequent denial of him. As we reflect on these heart-tugging scenarios, is it any wonder that Jesus, knowing what he would soon be facing, reacted with sorrowful incredulity when he found his dearest disciples and friends asleep when he asked them to keep watch with him?

As we review the events and intimate conversations Jesus had with his disciples before the chief priests and elders arrested him in the garden, aren't we cut to the heart when Jesus says, "My soul is overwhelmed with sorrow to the point of death"? We see the depth of his soul's agony when "he fell with his face to the ground and prayed, 'My Father, if it is possible, may this cup be taken from me. Yet not as I will, but as you will.'" Clearly, we see Jesus is wrestling with the knowledge of what he must suffer to reconcile the world to God. He knows what he will be called on to endure, and he begs his heavenly Father to spare him. Yes, Jesus asks to be spared, but there's more here for us to glean from the heartrending scene.

Jesus not only requests that his disciples share the burden with him through prayer, but he ties together the "watch and pray" spiritual truth for them. "Watch and pray so that you will not fall into temptation. The spirit is willing, but the flesh is weak." He wants them to understand the spiritual connection between submitting themselves to God's perfect will and humbling themselves before God in humble reliance and prayer so they can endure whatever comes next. Jesus understood what we frequently don't. He knew that to find peace in troubled moments and times of great temptation, we must fall before God (literally or figuratively) and cry out in prayer. We would do best in those perilous times when we feel overwhelmed or sorrowful or tempted beyond what we believe we can endure to follow the example Jesus set in the moments of his direst need. Watch and pray, and then offer up the prayer that never fails: "Thy will be done."

※ ※ ※

Jesus' evening of torment before his arrest is instructive for us as believers today. We are allowed the priceless privilege of gaining an insider's view of our Savior's battle against temptation. We read how even mere hours before his suffering began, Jesus continued to shepherd his flock with wisdom, warnings, and rebukes. He truly set aside his own interests and looked to the eternal interests of his disciples. Jesus could have set the disciples straight by reminding them of what he was soon to endure and suffer leading to the cross. But he didn't. Even when the weight (the sin of the world) of what Jesus was soon to experience at the hands of evil men was upon him, he set aside his own burdens to humbly meet his disciples' needs.

As we prayerfully reflect on all that took place between Jesus and his disciples in the Garden of Gethsemane, we do well to meditate on Jesus' example and imitate his instructions, "Watch and pray so that you will not fall into temptation. The spirit is willing, but the flesh is weak." Jesus knew what he would be facing in the hours that loomed before him. Jesus also understood what his disciples would face in the coming hours, days, weeks, and months. He wanted them to be ready, so he set the example by bowing before his heavenly Father and praying for God's will to be done.

We can also take this lesson to heart as we face our own seasons of intense suffering and sorrow. Do we take Jesus' instructive words seriously and model them in our lives when we feel overwhelmed by circumstances or are tempted to give way to sin? As we learn to humbly rely on God day in and day out, come what may, and make this humble reliance upon God be our default response to suffering and sorrow, then we truly emulate Jesus' posture in the garden. Watch and pray. Thy will be done.

My Heart's Cry to You, O Lord

Father, I'm often tempted to despair when circumstances become so overwhelming that I want to give up. I know I don't have the strength to fight against the trials that come against me. Help me to trust in your faithful supply of moment-by-moment grace. Help me to turn quickly to you and pray for the grace and strength to endure whatever you allow into my life. I know your will is perfect even when I don't understand what's happening. Give me the inner peace to accept your will and to trust that you will provide grace and the way of escape in moments of unbelief and temptation. I love you, Lord. Amen.

The Humble Life in Everyday Life

1. **Humility before God.** *"My Father, if it is possible, may this cup be taken from me. Yet not as I will, but as you will."* Spend time each day confessing any areas of unwillingness to submit to God's will in your life. Pray for God's sustaining grace and peace to fill your heart despite any fear you may be experiencing.

2. **Humility before others.** *Then he returned to his disciples and found them sleeping. "Couldn't you men keep watch with me for one hour?"* Be mindful of the needs

of others throughout this week. Pray that God will equip you to trust him for your needs and reach out selflessly to meet the needs of others who are hurting and suffering.

3. **Humility of heart.** *"Watch and pray so that you will not fall into temptation. The spirit is willing, but the flesh is weak."* Take time to prayerfully reflect on the past week, remembering any moments when the temptation to give up almost overwhelmed you. Was your default response one of trust and humble reliance on God's ability to protect and deliver you? If not, pray for God to strengthen your faith as you meet future challenges and trials.

Chapter 9

The Humble Have a Right
View of Jesus' Deity

But the Pharisees went out and plotted how they might kill Jesus.

Aware of this, Jesus withdrew from that place. A large crowd followed him, and he healed all who were ill. He warned them not to tell others about him. This was to fulfill what was spoken to prophet Isaiah:

"Here is my servant whom I have chosen,
the one I love, in whom I delight;
I will put my Spirit on him,
and he will proclaim justice to the nations.
He will not quarrel or cry out;
no one will hear his voice in the streets.
A bruised reed he will not break,
and a smoldering wick he will not snuff out,
till he has brought justice through to victory.
In his name the nations will put their hope."

Matthew 12:14–21

Once again, we find Jesus wrangling with the Pharisees' blatant hypocrisy as they reminded him that his disciples were doing something unlawful on the Sabbath by plucking heads of grain to eat. Jesus answers them saying, "The Son of Man is Lord of the Sabbath" (Matt. 12:8). After this, Jesus went into the synagogue and healed a man with a withered hand. Again, the Pharisees challenge him and Jesus answers them:

> "If any of you has a sheep and it falls into a pit on the Sabbath, will you not take hold of it and lift it out? How much more valuable is a person than a sheep! Therefore it is lawful to do good on the Sabbath." (Matt. 12:11–12)

Jesus is constantly pointing out the legalism they place above mercy and doing what is right.

In today's text, we read that after these two verbal altercations, Jesus knew the Pharisees had begun plotting to kill him. What did Jesus do in response to this threat? He withdrew from that place. The large crowd followed him, however, yet Jesus healed all who were ill. He then told the crowd not to speak to others about him. It's interesting to note that Jesus clearly responded to his accusers by telling them of his Son of Man status, yet he never sought the acclaim or status that title would give him. Instead, we see Jesus doing what he came to do: humbly serve. Jesus cared about the lost, the hurting, and the outcast. His every word and action declares this truth. He directly faces off with his ungodly accusers with simple facts. He challenges their self-righteous spirit with a greater truth that it is lawful to do good on the Sabbath. Then he leaves them to their own evil devices and goes to another place to continue his good work.

Now, we get an insider's view on God the Father's prophetic response from Isaiah 42:1–4, where the Father proclaims his love for his Son, Jesus. Matthew refers to the quotation from Isaiah noting that God is pleased with Jesus for his exemplary love and service to mankind. He punctuates his love, his delight, and then describes his servant's ministry to the hurting and the hopeless. What a contrast between the proud self-righteous Pharisees and Jesus' humble selflessness. This scene is but one of the stark but beautiful contrasts between spiritual darkness and light. How can we not respond ourselves in abject humility when faced with such a divine example of Jesus' deity as he loved and served the neediest of all?

※ ※ ※

As we take time to study this Gospel story about Jesus' interactions with the Pharisees, we can't help but be struck by how he conducts himself with both those who oppose him and those who come to him in need. Jesus was perfectly sinless, one-hundred percent God in the form of man. He is the Savior of humanity and yet the humble approach with which he carries out his divine destiny is awe inspiring. It's also humbling to every one of us for whom he spilt his precious blood in payment for our sins. As we meditate on this powerful passage where Jesus speaks boldly yet with perfect composure to those who continually challenge him and his authority, we're blessed with the example we should follow when we are similarly opposed and challenged.

How might we best glean the lesson Jesus would have us learn here? Might we contemplate more fully that Jesus chose to honor and obey his heavenly Father's will despite the opposition that faced him (and the price that obedience would cost him)? How might we take to heart Jesus' laser-focused intent to ease the suffering of the lost and needy who came to him? How might we be moved by the prophetic message from God the Father toward his servant Jesus as shared in Isaiah?

Our challenge then, is to read, meditate, and prayerfully ask God to enable us to understand Jesus' humility more fully, which was a living rebuke toward the Pharisees who desired public recognition and respect but without the selflessness and other-oriented service Jesus displayed. It's a marvel to reflect on these precious real-life conversations and scenarios that took place in Jesus' time. Let's take the time necessary to read this portion of Scripture with reverence and reflect on Jesus' deity and how much the Father loved him.

My Heart's Cry to You, O Lord

Father, help me to quiet my heart and mind and sit before you, meditating on the deity of Jesus. Help me to more fully understand that Jesus was fully God and fully man as he walked on earth. Give me a deeper appreciation for all he endured and suffered on my behalf. I want to follow in his footsteps and bring honor to you, Father, to Jesus, and the Holy Spirit as I endeavor to speak, serve, and minister to those around me. Open my eyes and let me see the divine wonder and eternal loveliness of the Trinity. Let me see your glory today, I pray. Amen.

The Humble Life in Everyday Life

1. **Humility before God.** *"Here is my servant whom I have chosen, the one I love, in whom I delight; I will put my Spirit on him, and he will proclaim justice to the nations."* Prayerfully reread this portion of Scripture each day and reflect on the love and delight of the Father toward the Son. This week, contemplate how you might humbly follow Jesus' perfect example of putting others' welfare before his own as you seek to love and serve those with whom you come into contact.

2. **Humility before others.** *"A bruised reed he will not break, and a smoldering wick he will not snuff out, till he has brought justice through to victory. In his name the nations will put their hope."* Each evening this week, take a few minutes to prayerfully reflect on the day and ask God to make you sensitive to those who are in need and hurting around you. Then make practical plans to ease the suffering as best you can.

3. **Humility of heart.** *"He will not quarrel or cry out; no one will hear his voice in the streets."* When faced with opposition for your faith, be intentional not to overreact or become angry at others when they challenge you. Rather, ask God to give you a heart of compassion to all, and then commit to pray for them to come to saving faith in Jesus.

Chapter 10

The Humble Submit with Simple Faith

People were bringing little children to Jesus for him to place his hands on them, but the disciples rebuked them. When Jesus saw this, he was indignant. He said to them, "Let the little children come to me, and do not hinder them, for the kingdom of God belongs to such as these. Truly I tell you, anyone who will not receive the kingdom of God like a little child will never enter it." And he took the children in his arms, placed his hands on them and blessed them.

Mark 10:13–16

In this Gospel account, we see how people were bringing children to Jesus for his blessing. Imagine being one of those children who sat on his lap and received that blessing! The disciples, however, thought Jesus was being bothered by all this. He had enough going on already to start handing out blessings to these kids.

But once again, we see how Jesus turns this moment into another lesson for his disciples, for the parents of those children, and for us today. "The kingdom of God belongs to such as these." In fact, not only does it belong to the little children, but they're the only ones who can enter it! He was angry with the disciples for trying to keep the children from him.

They felt the little ones weren't worth his trouble, but Jesus sees those innocent eyes and hearts and longs for that simple, trusting faith for all his children—including the grown-up ones. He knows how complicated our lives get the older we become, the more years we live. Children don't worry about how they're going to dress themselves or what they're going to eat. They trust that these things will be provided for them. Likewise, Jesus wants us to trust that God will provide for our needs. If we truly trust our heavenly Father, then we can experience the same unfettered joy we see when children are at play. Our hearts can be as light as theirs if we could only stop worrying so much about everything.

But why did the disciples even entertain in their hearts and minds that Jesus would be too busy or uninterested in these little ones? Clearly, they continued to battle with their desire for Jesus to reign as the coming king over the nation, which meant rescue from the oppression of the Roman Empire. Like us sometimes, they wanted Jesus to be the god of their own imaginations, not who he told them he was. They hoped Jesus had come to stop their suffering and release them from the tyranny of Rome. In this way, I can relate to the disciples' desires. I often hope and pray that God will rescue me and others from suffering, grief, and sorrow. But, like the disciples, I too must remind myself of his divine purpose and humbly submit to Jesus and rest in him in faith.

In closing, we can observe a beautiful "amen" to this poignant scene as we read what Jesus did next: "And he took the children in his arms, placed his hands on them and blessed them." Here we see that Jesus, busy and exhausted though he must have been, was never too distracted or weary to reach out and love these little ones. The lesson here is simple:

Jesus loves me, this I know, for the Bible tells me so.

Little ones to him belong; they are weak, but he is strong.

Yes, Jesus loves me. Yes, Jesus loves me. Yes, Jesus loves me.

The Bible tells me so.

※ ※ ※

Jesus was clearly trying to get his disciples to understand what the heart of a true believer should look like. He used this moment to show them that genuine faith is simply believing and humbly submitting to him. These parents knew enough to want Jesus to bless their children. It was the disciples who missed the mark by rebuking them for trying to do so.

Reading this Gospel story, I'm incredulous that these men who walked and talked with Jesus still didn't understand his heart. And yet, if I'm honest, how often do I miss the mark and assume I know what Jesus wants me to do? Am I too frequently critical of others' "simple faith" when it doesn't meet my spiritual standards? Do I assume the position of judging what's best instead of taking on a spirit of humility and compassion? These are hard (and spiritually telling) questions I must ask myself.

As we study Jesus' response to the disciples, we learn about the value of a humble heart that trusts in God just as children trust their parents. We read how Jesus clearly admonished the disciples while reminding them that only those with a childlike faith will enter the kingdom of heaven. Again, we must prayerfully ask ourselves if we have that heart of humility that doesn't need to understand everything that happens to us, that doesn't need to take control of every situation, or that insists on doing things our way. Rather, Jesus entreats us to step off the throne of our lives and walk in complete trust and faith in our heavenly Father.

My Heart's Cry to You, O Lord

Father, I need to return to the childlike faith I once had as a new believer. I remember my newfound faith in you and how I simply and humbly believed. I didn't need to have all my questions answered. I didn't need to be in control of my life. I simply believed in you and trusted you would take care of me. And you always have cared for me just as your word promises. Help me reignite that simple childlike faith in my heart. Give me your wisdom and understanding to know, really know, that all I need is you. Amen.

The Humble Life in Everyday Life

1. **Humility before God.** *"Truly I tell you, anyone who will not receive the kingdom of God like a little child will never enter it."* Take time this week to recall your early days as a new believer in Christ. Prayerfully consider how joyful you were in those first weeks and months of being a Christian, knowing that God had called you to himself for all eternity.

2. **Humility before others.** *"Truly I tell you, anyone who will not receive the kingdom of God like a little child will never enter it."* Each day, take a few moments to think about the interactions you've had with others. Did you exhibit a humble, compassionate spirit toward your family, friends, and coworkers? Pray for sensitivity and a selfless spirit to consistently reign inside your heart.

3. **Humility of heart.** *"Truly I tell you, anyone who will not receive the kingdom of God like a little child will never enter it."* Ask God to clothe you with a humble,

childlike spirit that simply trusts and obeys. Pray for the wisdom to be entirely dependent on God all day, every day. Ask him to cleanse your heart of any pride and self-reliance that hinders your relationship with him and others.

Chapter 11

The Humble Trust in God's Plans

"Therefore, I tell you, do not worry about your life, what you will eat or drink; or about your body, what you will wear. Is not life more than food, and the body more than clothes? Look at the birds of the air; they do not sow or reap or store away in barns, and yet your heavenly Father feeds them. Are you not much more valuable than they? Can any one of you by worrying add a single hour to your life?

"And why do you worry about clothes? See how the flowers of the field grow. They do not labor or spin. Yet I tell you that not even Solomon in all his splendor was dressed like one of these. If that is how God clothes the grass of the field, which is here today and tomorrow is thrown into the fire, will he not much more clothe you— you of little faith? So do not worry, saying, 'What shall we eat?' or 'What shall we drink?' or 'What shall we wear?' For the pagans run after all these things, and your heavenly Father knows that you need them. But seek first his kingdom and his righteousness, and all these things will be given to you as well. Therefore do not worry about tomorrow, for tomorrow will worry about itself. Each day has enough trouble of its own."

Matthew 6:25–34

Jesus enters into his discourse about not worrying immediately after issuing his warning to the disciples on the practical and spiritual impossibility of serving two masters. He wants them to understand that God is their perfect provider no matter what the circumstance. Thus he opens this lesson by pointing out in no uncertain terms why they must choose to serve either God or money. "No one can serve two masters. Either you will hate the one and love the other, or you will be devoted to the one and despise the other. You cannot serve both God and money" (Matt. 6:24). In other words, Jesus is encouraging them to trust God to meet their needs and see him as their always present and faithful provider. Next comes the "therefore," which is *there for* us to take special note of what Jesus says about the futility and sinfulness of worry. It's as if Jesus is contrasting our temptation to put our faith in our material resources (money) instead of being dependent on God to care for us.

Jesus continues by describing the beauty and careful design of God's created world and all its creatures. He elaborates on how God provides for these wondrous animals and plants that neither "labor or spin," and yet he clothes each one according to his splendid design. Here we see Jesus creating a picture of natural wonder and the beauty created and cared for by God himself. Jesus further explains that these marvelously designed natural creations were perfectly planned by God to grow, thrive, and flourish in this world. His point? How much more will God care for each of us as his beloved children who are far more valuable than these?

Jesus goes into even greater detail as he contrasts the short lifespan of these flowers, as God's care is intricate and complete for them even though each one is "here today and tomorrow is thrown into the fire." The brevity of their existence doesn't matter. God's loving care is always complete no matter how long a lifespan. Again, this is another illustration for the disciples to ponder because they are to live their lives as images of him, designed by God for his good and glorious purposes.

Finally, after homing in on the design and existence of the natural created world, Jesus chastises the disciples for their unbelief and worrying by comparing them to those who don't know God and anxiously run after these material things. Jesus exhorts his followers to "seek first his kingdom and his righteousness, and all these things will be given you as well." Jesus promises them that since God is always faithful to his children, he will provide for their every need. It's foolish to worry about tomorrow because "each day has enough trouble of its own." Here, Jesus ends his lesson on choosing to trust God for our every need rather than sink into the downward cycle of constant worry and fear. Every day we can observe the natural created world as Jesus taught so that we have a constant reference and reminder of God's omnipotent and sovereign care over his entire created world.

※ ※ ※

Let's take note of the chronology of this text from Jesus. First, he tells his followers that it's impossible to serve both God and money. Impossible, for we'll either love the one and hate the other. Why? Consider this, if we choose to follow money, it will get in the way of our service to Christ both practically and spiritually. One way or another, the pursuit of money versus the pursuit of Christ will run into conflict. In truth, we all understand that we're limited beings with limited time, energy, and skills. What we must ask ourselves is this: Whom will we serve? We have to choose.

In his discourse on the beauty and care of the natural created world and how God so intricately planned and designed each animal, plant, and all other natural resources, Jesus provides a picture of God's grand scheme of planning, creating, and caring for all his creations. He then gently rebukes his disciples for their lack of faith as they worry about how their needs will be met. Again, he contrasts God's perfect love toward his beloved children with his perfect provision for his lesser creations.

Did the disciples grasp the message? Did they understand the stark contrast between their loyalty to God versus a divided one with the pursuit of money (or perhaps their own cherished plans, goals, and dreams)? Do we understand what Jesus was conveying here? He wants us to abandon our worry in favor of trusting God with our future, our daily needs, and our moment-by-moment journey through this life. Yes, worry is a mighty foe, one that every person battles against at times. But as we study this passage of Scripture carefully, we not only see the futility of worry itself, but we can also discern how it's the humble in heart who more easily trust in God's perfect provision. It's the proud of heart who are determined to meet their needs apart from God's help. It's the proud of heart who stubbornly press their way into situations that will benefit them alone. It's the proud of heart who refuse to bow the knee to God and willingly (even happily) submit to his perfect plan for their lives. Because of this independent stance, worry is a constant plague for these wayward souls.

May we take to heart Jesus' words here and humbly submit ourselves to God's perfect plans for us day by day, hour by hour, and minute by minute. May we each lay down our pervasive willfulness that breeds what God opposes: a prideful, independent spirit. Instead, may we wisely humble ourselves under his protective, mighty hand and allow him to guide us, though it may take us places we sometimes prefer not to travel.

My Heart's Cry to You, O Lord

Father, I struggle so much with worry. I admit that my battle against worrying is in part because I'm afraid I won't get my own way. I want certain things to come to pass, and I worry they might slip away if I don't take charge of situations, people, or the uncertain tomorrow. Help me to let go of the things of this world and seek you first and foremost. Let my greatest desire be to honor you by trusting you—pleasing you and not myself. Help me to lay down my prideful endeavors at the foot of the cross and leave them there. Give me a renewed spirit and humble heart that seeks your glory alone. Amen.

The Humble Life in Everyday Life

1. **Humility before God.** *"But seek first his kingdom and his righteousness, and all these things will be given to you as well."* Spend time each morning and evening this week reading and meditating on these passages. Write down the contrasts between God's perfect provision for both his natural created world and his beloved children who are much more valuable. Pray that God will help you experience perfect peace as you drink in this marvelous truth.

2. **Humility before others.** *"So do not worry, saying, 'What shall we eat?' or 'What shall we drink?' or 'What shall we wear?' For the pagans run after all these things, and your heavenly Father knows that you need them."* This week, take time to reflect on your recent attitudes and actions. How do your choices demonstrate your calling to pursuing the honor of God above all else? Ask God to reveal to you if your priorities honor him or focus on your own selfish gain.

3. **Humility of heart.** *"Therefore do not worry about to-morrow, for tomorrow will worry about itself. Each day has enough trouble of its own."* Spend time studying this section of Scripture, and then write down any areas of your life where you're prone to worry. Ask God to clothe you with a humble, dependent, and trusting heart in him alone.

Chapter 12

The Humble Desire God's Will above Their Own

Then Jesus said to his disciples, "Whoever wants to be my disciple must deny themselves and take up their cross and follow me. For whoever wants to save their life will lose it, but whoever loses their life for me will find it. What good will it be for someone to gain the whole world, yet forfeit their soul? Or what can anyone give in exchange for their soul? For the Son of Man is going to come in his Father's glory with his angels, and then he will reward each person according to what they have done."

Matthew 16:24–27

Before we reach this passage in Matthew's Gospel, the Pharisees and the Sadducees demanded a sign from heaven, which led Jesus to warn his disciples to beware of these religious hypocrites. After this, Jesus asks his disciples to tell him who the people are saying he is. They answer that some believe he was John the Baptist raised from the dead, and some said he was Elijah or even Jeremiah. Then, in one of his more shining moments, Peter declares, "You are the Messiah, the Son of the living God." Jesus called Peter blessed because God alone revealed this truth to him.

All these conversations set the stage for Jesus to share yet another hard truth to them: how he must go to Jerusalem, suffer many things, be killed, and on the third day rise again. Then, back to his old zealous self, Peter exclaims, "Never, Lord! This shall never happen to you!" In what must have felt like a slap in the face, Peter hears Jesus say, "Get behind me, Satan! You are a stumbling block to me; you do not have in mind the concerns of God, but merely human concerns." Jesus then uses this moment to explain what it's all about, which is completely the opposite of what any of us would be thinking: "Whoever wants to be my disciple must deny themselves and take up their cross and follow me."

Here, Jesus plainly tells his disciples what's going to happen to him in the coming days: He's going to be crucified at the hands of the chief priests and the teachers of the law. In order to save their lives, Jesus says, they need to lose them. It doesn't matter if they gain the whole world if they lose their souls. Is this really what these disciples signed up for? To submit themselves to Roman execution by willingly going to the cross? It was bad enough that Jesus was saying he was going to be handed over to be killed, but that he was saying they had to follow him to that death? Was this what it means to be a disciple of Jesus?

Yes, it will cost them everything.

But there is more to the story. Yes, Jesus will be killed, but he also says that he will rise again on the third day. While they're wondering if this is another one of his parables and maybe he doesn't mean any of this literally, he says, "The Son of Man is going to come in his Father's glory with his angels, and then he will reward each person according to what they have done." Jesus' great love for his disciples and their eternal welfare compels him to teach them the whole truth of what being a disciple will cost each of them. They will have to choose to lose their lives one decision, one choice, one step at a time, just as Jesus did. In complete submission to God's will, the disciples will have to follow in Jesus' steps.

※ ※ ※

As we contemplate Jesus' words about what it costs to follow him, he clearly wants us to understand that only by giving away our lives will we find it. Step by step, choice by choice, we must seek to keep our eyes on the goal of fulfilling the greater eternal purposes for which God has created us.

Jesus painfully understood what God expected him to accomplish for the salvation of the world. What more powerful lesson was there for the disciples to learn than by watching their Lord and soon to be Savior willingly walk to his death in humility to God's perfect plan?

Like our Savior, we too must be willing to say no to our selfish desires, our self-centered plans, and seek to serve and honor him by cultivating a heart of humble submission to whatever road God has prepared for us to travel upon. How often do we balk at minor changes in our plans? How frequently do we silently complain in our hearts when someone upsets our cherished ideas and goals? May each of us meditate on the high cost that Christ paid for our sins and how he willingly subjected himself to the suffering inflicted on him by evil. Our hearts should desire to do whatever we can to honor and serve him, even though it could cost us everything we hold dear. As his beloved children, may we all choose daily—and choose rightly—to offer ourselves as living sacrifices to him who created us before the foundation of the world, who sustains us moment-by-moment, and who gives us the secure and holy hope of life eternal in his blessed presence.

My Heart's Cry to You, O Lord

Father, I am keenly aware that I often struggle against submitting myself to your plans when they conflict with mine. Help me, Lord. Give me your divine wisdom and resilient grace to choose to submit myself to your will. Remind me of Jesus' sacrifice on the cross for my sins. Never let me forget that he suffered on my behalf so that I can enjoy eternal life in his glorious presence. Oh, Lord, help me to see all of life through the lens of eternity so I don't fall short of accomplishing the good deeds of service you established for me before the foundation of the world. Amen.

The Humble Life in Everyday Life

1. **Humility before God.** *"Whoever wants to be my disciple must deny themselves and take up their cross and follow me."* Ask God to reveal to you any areas of your life where you have resisted obeying him. Prayerfully spend time today asking God to create in you a humble heart that is willingly submissive to his perfect will no matter the cost to you personally.

2. **Humility before others.** *"For whoever wants to save their life will lose it, but whoever loses their life for me will find it."* Spend time today in introspection and prayer about the patterns in your life regarding how you make short- and long-term decisions. Are you eager (or at least willing) to set aside your cherished ideas and goals in favor of serving God and others? Do you cheerfully set aside your plans when someone's need is presented to you? If not, how can you do better?

3. **Humility of heart.** *"What good will it be for some-one to gain the whole world, yet forfeit their soul? Or what can anyone give in exchange for their soul?"* With journal in hand, take time to prayerfully consider your life goals. Are these personal goals in line with God's commandment to go and make disciples of all nations? Can you honestly say you're giving your best (by way of talents, gifts, and material possessions) to witness to the kingdom of God and serve others in love and humility?

Chapter 13

The Humble Overcome Evil with Good

"You have heard that it was said, 'Love your neighbor and hate your enemy.' But I tell you, love your enemies and pray for those who persecute you, that you may be children of your Father in heaven. He causes his sun to rise on the evil and the good, and sends rain on the righteous and the unrighteous. If you love those who love you, what reward will you get? Are not even the tax collectors doing that? And if you greet only your own people, what are you doing more than others? Do not even pagans do that? Be perfect, therefore, as your heavenly Father is perfect."

Matthew 5:43–48

In Jesus' message from the Sermon on the Mount, he spotlights different topics and life scenarios for his listeners to hear and understand. He first teaches the Beatitudes before moving on to being salt and light in the unbelieving world and fulfilling the law. He then gives directives on such difficult life situations such as murder, adultery, divorce, oath-making, and the commonly taught but unloving axiom of an eye for an eye, before finally addressing loving one's enemies. In this single lesson, Jesus highlights many life challenges in a concise and pointed manner.

Jesus tells his listeners that in the past they had been told it was acceptable to love their neighbor and hate their enemy. But then he takes that and turns it on its head by admonishing them to love their enemies and to pray for those who persecute them so that they may be children of their Father in heaven. This two-part emphasis of loving our enemies and praying for those who persecute us must have confused his audience. From their human perspective, the only natural recourse that makes sense is to love those who love you and hate those who are your enemies. But once again, Jesus wanted to give us yet another glimpse into what a tiny bit of heaven on earth might look like if they followed his commands and sought to live and love others as children of the Father of light.

He continues by sharing examples of the common grace that God bestows on all people, not just those of faith, saying how God graciously "causes his sun to rise on the evil and the good, and sends rain on the righteous and the unrighteous." Then Jesus shifts his emphasis from God's common grace and goodness toward all to a comparison of how even tax collectors and pagans love those who love them. He quite intentionally uses tax collectors (despised as traitors to the Jewish people) and pagans (those who worship false gods) to make his teaching point hit home. Even these "sinners" know how to love those who love them. But Jesus expects his followers to go against the worldly grain and love those they would normally and naturally hate.

Seamlessly, Jesus then ties up this lesson by saying, "Be perfect, therefore, as your heavenly Father is perfect." Jesus instructs those with ears to hear that they need to go further in love than their unbelieving counterparts. They must seek to be "perfect" in love as God is by overcoming evil with good through the practical steps of first loving their enemies and then praying for those who persecute them. While no human can be defined as "perfect," Jesus raises the bar of human standards to God's perfect standard of holiness. Without even using the word *humility*, Jesus describes how believers can exemplify this perfect love by taking on the mantle of a humble and contrite heart, even in the face of persecution. We are to love our enemies and pray for those who persecute us, which means we entrust ourselves and our well-being into the faithful hands of God no matter how ill we're treated, how despised we may be, or how much rejection we may be called on to endure.

※ ※ ※

Let's be honest. It's humbling indeed to choose to love those we view as enemies and then take it a step further by praying for those who persecute us by treating us with unkindness or even rejection. To make an even more significant impact on those around us with whom we struggle to have unity and peace, we must seek to bless them and enrich their lives as we're able. Jesus instructs us to overcome evil with good and thereby break the cycle of sin and pain through his abundant grace and strength.

Truly, it's a great beginning to love our enemies and pray for their spiritual and physical well-being. But we can go further and learn to perfect our love as God loves us by seeking our enemies' best in the various practical ways of their lives. Let's invite the Lord to show us how we might make a blessed difference in their lives that will lighten their load, lift their spirits, and demonstrate God's love toward them. Can we make a meal? Offer to babysit? Share produce from our garden? Offer a cup of coffee or a glass of cold water? Can we show compassion, mercy, and kindness? Yes, to all the above. Simple gestures.

Small steps. It all can spark the flame of unconditional love, and who knows what Jesus can do with it once the heart is ignited?

As we prayerfully seek the Lord's guidance on creative ways to demonstrate our commitment to overcome evil with good, we can begin by knowing our own hearts. Do we seek to nurture a heart of humility with others? Even when we've been wronged? Difficult as this may be, Jesus issues the challenge to love our enemies and pray for them as he reminds us that we are children of the Father and should live accordingly. Let's start this spiritually dynamic journey by first prayerfully seeking to forgive others' sins against us and leave these hurtful offenses in the hands of God. Then, let's be intentional in our efforts to demonstrate humble, compassionate love toward them through consistent prayer and carefully tailored acts of service to bless them. Love your enemies. Pray for those who persecute you. Then seek to bless them in every way you can.

My Heart's Cry to You, O Lord

Father, help me to quickly forgive those who sin against me. Give me your unconditional love toward those who may seek to hurt me. Please bestow on me the wisdom and understanding I need to navigate difficult challenges with others. Give me the strength to embrace a spirit of humility in all that I do and say. Guide my thoughts and prayers as I intercede on behalf of others and seek to bring blessing into their lives. Amen.

The Humble Life in Everyday Life

1. **Humility before God.** *"Be perfect, therefore, as your heavenly Father is perfect."* Seek to have clean accounts with all people. If you're struggling to forgive someone, ask the Lord to give you the supernatural grace to forgive

and then begin praying for that person each morning and evening. Look for one way to show practical love toward them this week.

2. **Humility before others.** *"But I tell you, love your enemies and pray for those who persecute you, that you may be children of your Father in heaven."* Take a step to move to love your enemies and pray for them by seeking to find ways to bless them through words of encouragement and tangible steps to make their lives richer.

3. **Humility of heart.** *"If you love those who love you, what reward will you get? Are not even the tax collectors doing that? And if you greet only your own people, what are you doing more than others? Do not even pagans do that?"* Pray for the Lord to create a fresh spirit of humility in your heart so that all that you think and do will bring honor and glory to God the Father. Locate several verses on humility to carry with you throughout the week for further reflection.

Chapter 14

The Humble Learn to Unburden Themselves

*"Come to me, all you who are weary and burdened, and
I will give you rest. Take my yoke upon you and learn
from me, for I am gentle and humble in heart, and you
will find rest for your souls. For my yoke is easy and my
burden is light."*

Matthew 11:28–30

Here we see Jesus offering his disciples an oh-so-
comforting lesson on how following the Father will assure them a life mercifully unburdened by the laws and
traditions of men that the rigid Pharisees taught and demanded.
Jesus wanted to release his followers from such burdensome
constraints. He knew that meticulously heeding these oppres-
sive rules did nothing to unburden the souls of those who tried
to uphold them.

Jesus wanted to bring consolation and comfort to everyone.
What a refreshing lesson this must have been to his listeners.
Now it must be noted that while Jesus was quick to reassure
his followers that once they gave their hearts to him and were
reborn by the Spirit, they would still be required to lay down
their lives every day in service to him.

We might well ask then if serving Jesus via a daily death is too self-burdensome in the extreme. No, says Jesus, because with him yoked together by our side, he carries the heaviest weight. When we are one with him in Spirit, born anew after his death and resurrection, Jesus provides us with true soul rest. Secure for eternity through his saving blood that he shed on the cross, each of us willingly lays down our lives in service to him as he teaches us his ways. As Jesus said, "Take my yoke upon you and learn from me, for I am gentle and humble in heart, and you will find rest for your souls."

We learn that as God's dearly beloved children we can rest secure in him, and no matter what we may be called on to sacrifice on this earth, his presence and power will equip and sustain us. We discover that Jesus, our Savior and redeemer, does not simply issue rules, mandates, and other weighty commands and then leave us on our own to accomplish them. Rather, Jesus provides a clear picture of what being one of his own looks like in real-life terms. Jesus assures his disciples that when they walk beside him, follow him, and submit to him, his yoke is indeed easy and his burden is light. Perhaps the most reassuring statement in this teaching are his first words to his weary and weak disciples, "Come to me, all you who are weary and burdened, and I will give you rest."

※ ※ ※

As we work through these passages, we learn that Jesus' idea of carrying a yoke that is easy and a burden that is light means something very different from what we might assume at first glance. Indeed, this passage is beautifully descriptive of what belonging to the Father as one of his own children merits: Rest for our souls for all eternity. What an immeasurable blessing this truth is to everyone who calls on the name of the Lord! But lest we neglect the fuller meaning and the debt we each owe to Jesus, we must remember that he demands that we offer up our lives to him day by day, hour by hour, moment by moment.

We dare not believe we can rest easy and live a life of ease after Jesus paid such a tremendous price for our sin. Never. Instead, Jesus ransomed us from the pain of the sin and death so that we might serve him throughout eternity. Our daily walk of service on earth with Jesus will be fraught with struggle, hardship, and pain. However, the shining and glorious truth is that Jesus will journey alongside us through this life. We are no longer on our own or bound to our sin as we once were. He promises to walk with us, to carry the greater burden for us, and to strengthen us in our service. Truly, with Jesus as our Savior and Lord, he takes on the bulk of the burdensome weight for us and works with us and through us, even in spite of our weaknesses. How humbling is this truth?

Jesus, our Lord, promises that his strength is enough for us. He tells us to unburden ourselves from the legalism that kills the soul by trusting in him for salvation and for the grace we need to live in service to him. As Jesus tells his disciples, "Take my yoke upon you and learn from me, for I am gentle and humble in heart, and you will find rest for your souls." Humbly, gratefully, we say, "Yes, Lord!"

My Heart's Cry to You, O Lord

Father, help me to keep my eyes fixed on you so that I am fully aware of your power and presence in my life to strengthen and sustain me. Give me the wisdom I need to follow close to you all my days and to give myself away in humble service to you. Show me your ways each and every day. Remind me that legalism kills the soul, but the Spirit gives life. Never let me forget Jesus' great sacrifice on the cross for my sins. Direct my steps one day at a time and help me to be thankful that Jesus is yoked alongside me and that I never have to journey through this life on my own. Amen.

The Humble Life in Everyday Life

1. **Humility before God.** *"Come to me, all you who are weary and burdened, and I will give you rest."* Remind yourself that Jesus invites you to enter into his rest for all of eternity and that legalism kills the spirit. Humble yourself before God this week and confess the times you tried to earn favor with God by following human laws and empty traditions.

2. **Humility before others.** *"Take my yoke upon you and learn from me, for I am gentle and humble in heart, and you will find rest for your souls."* This week, purpose to serve Jesus by serving others around you. Study Jesus' words about selfless service and place others' welfare above your own. Then journal your experiences at the end of the week.

3. **Humility of heart.** *"For my yoke is easy and my burden is light."* Prayerfully acknowledge to the Lord that you are completely dependent on him and his continual grace to serve him in this life. Then thank him for bearing the greater burden as you are yoked to your loving Savior and serve him day by day.

Chapter 15

The Humble are Full of Faith

A woman was there who had been subject to bleeding for twelve years. She had suffered a great deal under the care of many doctors and had spent all she had, yet instead of getting better she grew worse. When she heard about Jesus, she came up behind him in the crowd and touched his cloak, because she thought, "If I just touch his clothes, I will be healed." Immediately her bleeding stopped and she felt in her body that she was freed from her suffering.

At once Jesus realized that power had gone out from him. He turned around in the crowd and asked, "Who touched my clothes?"

"You see the people crowding against you," his disciples answered, "and yet you can ask, 'Who touched me?'"

But Jesus kept looking around to see who had done it. Then the woman, knowing what had happened to her, came and fell at his feet and, trembling with fear, told him the whole truth. He said to her, "Daughter, your faith has healed you. Go in peace and be freed from your suffering."

Mark 5:25–34

There are so many wonderful dimensions to this account of the woman with the bleeding disorder who sought out Jesus for healing. First, we need to understand that from a historical and societal perspective, this suffering woman was viewed as unclean and therefore was an outcast. As Mark's Gospel points out, she had gone from doctor to doctor seeking help and had spent all the money she had, yet still she suffered. Indeed, instead of finding some relief from her condition, she grew worse. We might well ask if her condition naturally deteriorated or did the doctors' treatments cause more harm than help? We don't know. What these passages do tell us, however, is that she was a woman in desperate circumstances in need of Jesus' healing touch.

Yet despite her need to meet Jesus (both physically and spiritually), getting to him was a problem. As an unclean woman by Jewish laws, she knew full well that no one would allow her to get that close to Jesus if they knew of her illness. It's also likely that most people in that town didn't know her because she would have by necessity been forced to exist outside the normal boundaries of life. By their customary laws and traditions, she truly could be considered a marked woman. What to do? This nameless woman, so full of faith, risked more rejection and even possible harm by attempting to covertly press her way just close enough to touch Jesus' garments. She said to herself, "If I just touch his clothes, I will be healed." So that's what she chose to do. She followed along, came up behind Jesus, and touched his cloak. What happened next? "Immediately her bleeding stopped and she felt in her body that she was freed from her suffering." Praise God!

While we can assume she quietly yet gratefully tried to disappear back into the crowd, Jesus realized healing power had gone out from him and he asked, "Who touched my clothes?" To which his disciples answered incredulously, "You see the people crowding against you and yet you can ask, 'Who touched me?'" But Jesus waited and watched because he wanted to assure the woman that she was truly healed (both physically and spiritually).

The woman was very likely terrified at what kind of rebuke she might receive given how others had treated her as one of the unclean for twelve years. Trembling with fear, she fell at Jesus' feet, and answered him truthfully. His response? "Daughter, your faith has healed you. Go in peace and be freed from your suffering." This nameless, but faithful woman, demonstrated the power of humility when she sought after Jesus as the only answer to her great need (both physical and spiritual). Praise God!

※ ※ ※

As we consider this lesson on the faith and humility it took for this nameless suffering woman to boldly follow after Jesus, we can learn so much about being in desperate straits yet still confident that Jesus can bring healing to us. Her faith was strong and robust despite the weakness of her body. We can assume that this twelve-year-long illness not only took a toll on her physical body but also on her mental and emotional well-being. Even in her abject distress, she knew Jesus was the only one who could help her.

This story is especially powerful when we consider how much rejection, suffering, and disappointment she had endured for more than a decade. Having exhausted every other feasible option available to her, this faithful woman found a way to get to Jesus despite the obstacles facing her from every turn. As we study her story, I wonder how often we courageously follow her stellar example to get to Jesus no matter what the cost to us personally. Are we willing to humble ourselves and risk upsetting others to follow him? Do we boldly find ways to get close to him in faith-filled expectation that only he can bring the healing we require?

Or are we more tempted to give up? Despite any (and all) troubling circumstances we face, this woman's bravery and her ever-so-humble heart knew that Jesus was the only answer to her problem. If only we would follow her example when faced with unthinkable—or seemingly unending—suffering from our human perspective and do all we can to get to Jesus. Once we meet him, we too can experience the same life-altering inner healing and peace.

My Heart's Cry to You, O Lord

Father, I'm overwhelmed and wearied by my current circumstances. In my heart and soul, I know you alone are the one who can bring restoration and healing to me. I also realize that my faith has been faltering of late. I've been distracted by my pain and discouraged because I've tried everything I know to alleviate these problems. Please clothe me with a spirit of humility and dependent trust. Help me to lean on you for my daily sustenance and strength to continue forward until you choose to bring relief to me. Amen.

The Humble Life in Everyday Life

1. **Humility before God.** *"Daughter, your faith has healed you. Go in peace and be freed from your suffering."* This week, remind yourself that Jesus tells you that you can rise above your circumstances and place all your hope and trust in him. Write down how God has met your needs in the past as a good reminder of his daily faithfulness and provision to you.

2. **Humility before others.** *"Daughter, your faith has healed you. Go in peace and be freed from your suffering."* Determine to speak words "full of faith" throughout the week. Purpose to fight against discouragement and despair and instead speak words that reveal your stalwart faith to others even in the midst of suffering.

3. **Humility of heart.** *"Daughter, your faith has healed you. Go in peace and be freed from your suffering."* Take time to pray each morning and evening about whatever you're struggling with and ask God to give you joyful hope as you wait on him to work his will in your life. Determine to get close to Jesus through time spent in Bible reading, prayer, and meditation.

Chapter 16

The Humble Follow Their Shepherd

"I am the good shepherd. The good shepherd lays down his life for the sheep. The hired hand is not the shepherd and does not own the sheep. So when he sees the wolf coming, he abandons the sheep and runs away. Then the wolf attacks the flock and scatters it. The man runs away because he is a hired hand and cares nothing for the sheep.

"I am the good shepherd; I know my sheep and my sheep know me—just as the Father knows me and I know the Father—and I lay down my life for the sheep. I have other sheep that are not of this sheep pen. I must bring them also. They too will listen to my voice, and they shall be one flock and one shepherd."

John 10:11–16

This passage of Scripture is replete with the comforting words that describe the responsibilities and burdens the good shepherd must bear as he fulfills his role to protect and save those under his care. Here, Jesus is speaking about the differences between the good shepherd who will lay his life down for his sheep as opposed to a mere hired hand (possibly referring to the Pharisees and false teachers) who run away as soon as there's trouble. Once the cost of shepherding becomes too high, they flee. But not Jesus, the only true and faithful shepherd. He gives his life for his sheep.

Jesus describes the stark contrast between the owner of the sheep as opposed to those who don't own them. The level of personal sacrifice is so distinct that it can mean the difference between life and death for the sheep. "So when he sees the wolf coming, he abandons the sheep and runs away. Then the wolf attacks the flock and scatters it. The man runs away because he is a hired hand and cares nothing for the sheep." As the good shepherd (Jesus) who is willing to lay down his life for his sheep, we read here how quickly the hired hand (the Pharisees and false teachers) will abandon the sheep to save themselves. Jesus wants his listeners to know the difference. He needs them to understand that they must know his shepherd's voice in order to follow him alone to be secure and eternally saved.

What a wonder and comfort it is for Jesus' sheep to recognize him, to listen to his voice, and then be joined with other sheep to make up the one flock (the church eternal) and the one shepherd (Jesus our Savior). We read here how Jesus explains that in similar fashion as to how the sheep know their true shepherd, the Father knows Jesus and Jesus knows the Father. In many passages in the New Testament, Jesus prays to the Father and the Father hears him. Jesus speaks to God the Father, and the Father answers him. Jesus knows the voice of his Father and does what he tells him to do. See the parallel here? The Father and Jesus are intimately connected—but in this case, Jesus is the Lamb of God who takes away the sins of the world.

Jesus reiterates how far his love will extend for his chosen sheep: "I lay down my life for the sheep." He then tells his listeners about the other sheep that he needs to gather and how they will be part of the church eternal and will listen to his voice and follow him. "I have other sheep that are not of this sheep pen. I must bring them also. They too will listen to my voice, and they shall be one flock and one shepherd." What a wondrous lesson this must have been for his disciples to hear about the depths of his love for each of them—his beloved flock.

※ ※ ※

There are so many takeaways for us as we ponder the depths of this beautiful message. We can take great comfort in Jesus' promise to rescue and protect his beloved sheep (we who are part of the church eternal). We're encouraged to know that we can hear his voice and distinguish him from false teachers who would distract us and lead us away from Christ. We also see how Jesus was willing to lay his life down for us while we were yet his enemies and sinners. Like the Pharisees of Jesus' day, the so-called hired hands (false teachers) of today continue to snare and entrap believers with half-truths and empty promises.

Jesus knows us and we know him. Jesus as our shepherd and Savior expects us to follow closely after him and to trust him entirely. Consider how Jesus, in the role of the good shepherd, cares for us and protects us from all harm. Let us reflect on his willingness to lay his life down to save us from our enemy of death. As he promised he would, Jesus laid down his life for his sheep, providing green pastures and peaceful waters forever.

As we contemplate Jesus' immense sacrifice for us, let us humble ourselves before him and purpose to follow him wherever he leads. How can we know where he wants us to go? We can hear his voice even today by following his command to renew our minds daily through reading Scripture, prayer, meditation, and memorizing his word. This is how we learn what the good shepherd expects of his sheep. We have sixty-six books in the Bible from which to draw all that we need for life and godliness in this danger-ridden world where wolves circle, hoping to devour us. But as Jesus promised, he is as much our good shepherd today as he was to his disciples over two thousand years ago.

My Heart's Cry to You, O Lord

Father, thank you for the wondrous promises you have given me as one of your beloved sheep. I am so thankful to be counted among your flock for all eternity. Help me to be diligent to spend time daily reading your word, praying, meditating, and memorizing your truth so that I can learn to better hear your voice. Give me divine wisdom and understanding so that I can distinguish between your truth and false teachers who would lead me astray. Clothe me with a humble, contrite heart that joyfully obeys your commands. Amen.

The Humble Life in Everyday Life

1. **Humility before God.** *"I am the good shepherd; I know my sheep and my sheep know me—just as the Father knows me and I know the Father—and I lay down my life for the sheep."* Set aside time every day this week to study Bible passages that describe the good shepherd and how he cares for his sheep. Journal any thoughts and insights you draw from these passages as it relates to how Jesus has cared for you during times of safety and times of unrest and danger.

2. **Humility before others.** *"I have other sheep that are not of this sheep pen. I must bring them also. They too will listen to my voice, and they shall be one flock and one shepherd."* Pray each day this week for those God

has called to repentance but have not yet asked for forgiveness. Commit to intercede for those in your life who don't know Jesus as their Savior and Lord. Resist the temptation to grow weary as you wait.

3. **Humility of heart.** *"I know my sheep and my sheep know me."* Begin a Bible study plan for yourself (if you're not already doing so). Start by memorizing one verse each week and keep a journal of all the verses you commit to memory. Make notations in your journal about how memorizing key passages of Scripture impacts your spiritual life for good and how this spiritual discipline better equips you to hear your shepherd's voice.

Chapter 17

The Humble Use Their Gifts for Kingdom Purposes

"Whoever can be trusted with very little can also be trusted with much, and whoever is dishonest with very little will also be dishonest with much. So if you have not been trustworthy in handling worldly wealth, who will trust you with true riches? And if you have not been trustworthy with someone else's property, who will give you property of your own?

"No one can serve two masters. Either you will hate the one and love the other, or you will be devoted to the one and despise the other. You cannot serve both God and money."

The Pharisees, who loved money, heard all this and were sneering at Jesus. He said to them, "You are the ones who justify yourselves in the eyes of others, but God knows your hearts. What people value highly is detestable in God's sight."

Luke 16:10–15

During the time when Jesus walked the earth, many associated monetary wealth with favor from God (as many still do today). Here we see Jesus debunking that misconception when the Pharisees sneer at him. As Luke says, they "loved money." Again, we see Jesus unveiling their hypocrisy, showing them just how far off they were in what they valued, which was "detestable in God's sight."

Jesus opens his teaching about the parable of the manager who wasn't doing a good job of looking after his master's accounts. However, the manager was shrewd enough to offer deals to his master's debtors so they would care for him when his master found out what he was doing and fired him. The master eventually finds out how shrewd the manager had acted in trying to protect himself and compliments him (though we don't know if he gave him back his job or not!).

Jesus ends his lesson discussing stewardship and priorities:

> "Whoever can be trusted with very little can also be trusted with much, and whoever is dishonest with very little will also be dishonest with much. So if you have not been trustworthy in handling worldly wealth, who will trust you with true riches?"

If we can't be trusted here on earth with what God blesses us, how can we be entrusted with "true riches"? True heavenly riches are not found in earthly monetary gain. Jesus wants his followers to search their own hearts and see how good a steward they have been. We are only temporary caretakers of any and all material gains God has blessed us with.

Then, in a surprising turn, Jesus likens money to a master we can actually serve—someone we can become attached to and ignore everyone else, including our true master. "No one can serve two masters. Either you will hate the one and love the other, or you will be devoted to the one and despise the other. You cannot serve both God and money." By saying this,

Jesus seeks to expose the hearts of his listeners, including the Pharisees. What do they value most? Is it money? Is it esteem? Is it both? We read here how the Pharisees responded to Jesus' clear teaching on heart priorities. "The Pharisees, who loved money, heard all this and were sneering at Jesus. He said to them, 'You are the ones who justify yourselves in the eyes of others, but God knows your hearts. What people value highly is detestable in God's sight.'" Jesus strips away the veneer of their false fronts and exposes them for all to see. They didn't love God; they loved money and the esteem of men. They were so full of pride they couldn't see how they weren't to be trusted with what is actually of great value: "true riches."

※ ※ ※

As we contemplate this message on money and stewardship, do we recognize ourselves in this section of Scripture? How often do we fall into the same trap as the Pharisees who cared only for outward appearances and for their physical comfort and well-being? Do we, like them, forget that everything we have been given by the Father is to be used and stewarded toward that which will make an eternal difference? Do we neglect to go to God in gratitude and humility to pray for his divine wisdom to determine how to best utilize these gifts? Are we sensitive to the needs of others so that we might generously give away some of our wealth to ease their burden and suffering?

These are hard questions, because we all struggle with the fine balance of distinguishing between what is enough to meet our needs (not our wants) with what we can give away. Jesus repeatedly admonished his followers throughout his time on earth to live selflessly, with an other-oriented mindset. Instead of lavishing on ourselves stuff we don't need, Jesus wants us to look to him as our master and the "true riches" we should be seeking from him. First and foremost, God wants our heart's allegiance. Once won, we will happily look for practical ways to live for Jesus and give generously to those in need in whatever form that may take.

My Heart's Cry to You, O Lord

Father, I admit that there are times when I fail to pray about how to use the wealth you have given me. I sometimes forget that I am simply a steward of your resources. I want to use everything I have and every talent and ability to further your kingdom. Help me to be wise, compassionate, and sensitive to the needs of others in my life. Give me your divine wisdom to know how to be a wise investor of money and other gifts, not so that I will have more to spend, but so that I have more to give away. Amen.

The Humble Life in Everyday Life

1. **Humility before God.** *"You are the ones who justify yourselves in the eyes of others, but God knows your hearts. What people value highly is detestable in God's sight."* Each morning this week, spend time looking up passages of Scripture that talk about humility and how God loves the humble but resists the proud. Write a few of these verses down and carry them with you to reflect on during the day.

2. **Humility before others.** *"No one can serve two masters. Either you will hate the one and love the other, or you will be devoted to the one and despise the other. You cannot serve both God and money."* Pray that God will reveal the needs of others in your life so that you can help them in practical ways. Continue to remind your-

self that everything belongs to God and is to be used to further his kingdom purposes. Pray to be both wise and selflessly generous.

3. **Humility of heart.** *"Whoever can be trusted with very little can also be trusted with much, and whoever is dishonest with very little will also be dishonest with much. So if you have not been trustworthy in handling worldly wealth, who will trust you with true riches?"* Journal each evening this week and reflect on the day's decisions regarding how you spent your time, your money, your resources. Ask God to reveal to you any areas where your heart wasn't obedient to his plan because it was divided between what you wanted and what he intended.

Chapter 18

The Humble Have Spiritual Well-Being

"Blessed are the poor in spirit,
for theirs is the kingdom of heaven.
Blessed are those who mourn,
for they will be comforted.
Blessed are the meek,
for they will inherit the earth.
Blessed are those who hunger and thirst for righteousness,
for they will be filled.
Blessed are the merciful,
for they will be shown mercy.
Blessed are the pure in heart,
for they will see God.
Blessed are the peacemakers,
for they will be called children of God.
Blessed are those who are persecuted because of righteousness,
for theirs is the kingdom of heaven."

Matthew 5:3–10

This beloved section of Scripture called the Beatitudes has been a comfort to countless believers through the centuries—and for good reason. This teaching from Jesus resonates with every individual because it offers more than temporary hope; it details in beautiful imagery the blessings that will be bestowed on God's children throughout eternity.

Here we read that Jesus is standing on a mountainside surveying those who have followed him. Then he sits down to teach his disciples and the masses. His physical posture of walking to a high place and then settling down to a sitting position before teaching implies that he is making himself comfortable. He isn't in a hurry. He is, however, eager to impart encouragement, hope, and eternal perspective to everyone in attendance. We can imagine him gazing at all those seated below him, moved to compassion by their needs—spiritual, physical, and emotional. Jesus looks out and with his shepherd-like devotion, he offers them eternal hope by communicating to them that he understands their daily plights. As he describes the varying emotions they experience day to day, he assures them of their eternal rewards in the coming kingdom.

Jesus identifies their struggles, and he encourages them to respond in ways that honor God through faith and trust. He knows that they are poor in spirit and that they are mourning. He commends those who are meek, who hunger and thirst for righteousness, who are merciful, who are pure in heart, who are peacemakers, and who are persecuted because of righteousness. He reassures them that God is watching and will recompense them in the coming kingdom for everything they suffer in this life. We can well imagine how moved they were as they listened to these words of encouragement. Jesus' tender approach toward their suffering, their discouragement, and their plight as individuals oppressed by the Romans must have lifted their hearts and renewed their hope.

Throughout this touching display of Jesus' shepherd-like care and love, we must note that in each of these specific areas, he described their spiritual well-being. "Blessing" is another word for overall well-being. Jesus wants them to rejoice and be glad that they belong to the Father and that he will make all things right in eternity. They can know Jesus as their peace. They can trust Jesus as their Lord and Savior. They can rest, inwardly confident that God oversees every moment of their lives. How Jesus must have won their hearts that day with his humility of loving, gentle exhortation. Here we truly see Jesus' shepherd's heart as he sits among his flock and speaks words that have encouraged generations of believers. Blessed are they! Blessed are we!

✳ ✳ ✳

As we ponder the possible responses from those in attendance that day, let's imagine ourselves sitting at Jesus' feet as he spoke these wonderful promises. How might we have responded as we listened to Jesus assuring us that we are indeed blessed because we belong to him? We are part of his flock for all eternity. In the here and now, as Jesus so succinctly stated, we may be poor in spirit, we may be mourning. But with every hurt and heartache, God promises us the blessing of spiritual well-being. We can learn to live in this precious space despite our difficult circumstances. Not only that, but Jesus wants us to know that our heart attitudes, our choices, and our reactions all have eternal repercussions. He wants us to know that the veil between this temporary life here on earth and eternal life in heaven is thin. How we choose to respond in the here and now to our suffering affects our eternal lives.

Jesus is here to offer us the opposite of what the world gives. He can help us overcome every trial, every ounce of suffering, every moment of grief and loss. He wants us to walk through this temporal life as imagers of his holy and perfect love. Here in this message, he gives us the visual blueprint of what overcoming the challenges of this life can look like. Whatever suffering we endure for righteousness' sake will be effectively null and void once we meet Jesus on the other side. But until then, we can rest in his promises, we can sit quietly in his presence, we can drink from the well that comes from Jesus and find ourselves satisfied and at peace. Blessed are we who know the wonder-working power of Jesus Christ as our beloved Lord and Savior, for the spiritual well-being of our souls can never be taken from us.

My Heart's Cry to You, O Lord

Father, help me to be wise enough to linger long in your word each day as I prayerfully contemplate your wondrous promises to me. Give me your eternal perspective on all that I face in my life today. Shower me with your grace so that whatever is happening all around me doesn't disturb the well-being of my soul. I belong to you. I am part of your flock. I thank you for choosing me to be part of your forever family. Your goodness and grace astound me. Use me to point others to you in the coming days, and may your Spirit guide my heart attitude, my works, my words, and my every breath. I want to lift your name high so that others see your glory. Amen.

The Humble Life in Everyday Life

1. **Humility before God.** *"Blessed are the pure in heart, for they will see God."* Each day this week, purpose to spend five minutes on the hour to give thanks for God's perfect provision for you. Give thanks by faith even before he answers your pleas for help and deliverance. Ask God to create in you a pure heart so that others might see his glory and honor him by trusting him.

106

2. **Humility before others.** *"Blessed are the merciful, for they will be shown mercy."* Spend time each day journaling your honest heart attitudes and struggles. Whether you're finding it difficult to love and serve others or struggling with being judgmental, ask God to help you treat everyone with mercy and kindness despite how they may treat you. Remind yourself that God is always watching, that he is our righteous judge, and that he will make all things right in eternity.

3. **Humility of heart.** *"Blessed are those who hunger and thirst for righteousness, for they will be filled."* Pray for a heart that increasingly hungers for righteousness. Ask God to give you a strong desire to know his word and to memorize his promises, knowing that they will protect and transform your life one thought at a time.

Chapter 19

The Humble Worship Jesus

While he was in Bethany, reclining at the table in the home of Simon the Leper, a woman came with an alabaster jar of very expensive perfume, made of pure nard. She broke the jar and poured the perfume on his head.

Some of those present were saying indignantly to one another, "Why this waste of perfume? It could have been sold for more than a year's wages and the money given to the poor." And they rebuked her harshly.

"Leave her alone," said Jesus. "Why are you bothering her? She has done a beautiful thing to me. The poor you will always have with you, and you can help them any time you want. But you will not always have me. She did what she could. She poured perfume on my body beforehand to prepare for my burial. Truly I tell you, wherever the gospel is preached throughout the world, what she has done will also be told, in memory of her."

Mark 14:3–9

This memorable passage of Scripture teaches us so many lessons in a single setting. Here we begin with Jesus who is visiting the home of Simon the Leper who was miraculously healed from his disease. The disciples are also in attendance when Mary (the sister of Martha and Lazarus) enters the scene. She was eager to demonstrate her great love for her Lord, and she did so by breaking the seal on a jar of perfume that cost the equivalent of a year's wages. Mary poured the perfume on Jesus' head to show her complete devotion to him. As a result, some Gospel accounts say that Judas (John 12:4) among others objected to her lavish generosity citing that this gift could be given to the poor.

Jesus rebuked him, saying, "Leave her alone. Why are you bothering her? She has done a beautiful thing to me. The poor you will always have with you, and you can help them any time you want. But you will not always have me. She did what she could. She poured perfume on my body beforehand to prepare for my burial." While Mary didn't intend to prepare Jesus' body for burial with her lavish expression of love, Jesus was foretelling his death. Here, we read how God orchestrated a beautiful intersection of love and devotion before Jesus was taken away from Mary and the disciples. What's most telling is the way in which Judas and some of the others revealed their callousness, even as they observed this poignant scene between Mary and Jesus. Their callous criticism of her wonderful and humbling act of love toward Jesus shows how hardened their hearts were at this moment.

Yet Jesus doesn't allow Mary to be embarrassed. Rather, he rebukes them to leave her alone. He knows Mary's pure heart only wanted to give expression to her complete devotion to him even though she broke that days' societal mores. Somehow, Mary understood this was a time for sacrificial worship of Jesus, and he commended her for it. He chided them for their criticism and indifference to her tender heart and public act of worship. How beautiful that Mary did not allow herself to be persuaded against this act of public extravagant love.

To further accentuate his point, Jesus concludes his rebuke with this promise: "Truly I tell you, wherever the gospel is preached throughout the world, what she has done will also be told, in memory of her." First of all, they were wrong to criticize her, and second, she will be remembered through eternity for what she did for him. Certainly, this entire exchange is about so much more than Mary's gift. It's yet another lesson about knowing one's heart and responding toward others in compassion, understanding, and unconditional love.

❋ ❋ ❋

As we contemplate this lesson, we learn so much from Mary's humble example as she set aside concerns about what others might think of her. As a woman in Jesus' time, she was socially constrained as to how close she could physically come to any man who wasn't her husband. Yet, with purity of heart, Mary felt compelled to express her worship of Jesus and ignored the rules of conduct. In other words, Mary threw off convention and felt a desperate need to be close to Jesus via her lavish worship of pouring the perfume over his head. In a way reminiscent of the way the woman with the issue of blood pressed through the crowds to touch Jesus' hem, so Mary pressed past the negative opinion of others to get to Jesus.

This brings us back to her humility of heart and how Mary willingly paid the price to worship Jesus (practically by pouring out the perfume and socially by disregarding how the disciples and others might react to her). She's an ideal model for us as to how we might worship Jesus so extravagantly. Do we willingly part with our riches and our material goods to meet the needs of others? Do we lay aside our preferences and plans to serve in Jesus' name? Do we joyfully submit to Jesus' example of conducting our lives so that in everything we are image-bearers of him? Do we love him first and foremost and lay down our lives as our spiritual act of service day in and day out? Each of these different ways of humbly worshiping Jesus can show a lost and dying world how much we love and adore him.

Real worship is not confined to our Sunday morning church services when we raise our voices in praise. Although worshiping through song is clearly part of our worship, the laying down of our lives every day is the truest worship. Perhaps some of our most impactful moments of worship in this life are those when Jesus calls us to trust and obey, and we do so without hesitation, without complaint, and without a word. In truth, real worship is birthed in our regenerated hearts, and its fruit continues to grow and flourish as long as we draw breath on earth.

My Heart's Cry to You, O Lord

Father, I want to give you all my praise and thanksgiving for saving me. I want to worship you with my heart and mind all the days of my life. I want my thoughts to continually rise in gratefulness for the goodness and grace with which you have filled my life. Clothe me, Lord, with a spirit of humility, compassion, and genuine love toward others. Remind me each morning that my truest act of worship is to lay down my life for you all day, every day. Give me a strong faith that seeks to trust and obey you no matter what difficulties and challenges I may face. Thank you, Lord, for you are good and worthy of all my worship, all my praise, for all my days. Amen.

The Humble Life in Everyday Life

1. **Humility before God.** *While he was in Bethany, reclining at the table in the home of Simon the Leper, a woman*

came with an alabaster jar of very expensive perfume, made of pure nard. She broke the jar and poured the perfume on his head. Spend time in prayer throughout the week asking God to reveal any areas of your life where you're not willing to submit to his will or to give him your all in worship. Ask yourself if there are specific areas in your life where you resist laying down your own preferences and plans to fully worship God with your life.

2. **Humility before others.** *Some of those present were saying indignantly to one another, "Why this waste of perfume? It could have been sold for more than a year's wages and the money given to the poor."* Ask yourself if you hold back worshiping God by refusing to give of your material goods or serve him sacrificially. Prayerfully consider what holds you back from humbly offering yourself and all you have in worshipful service to God.

3. **Humility of heart.** *"She did what she could. She poured perfume on my body beforehand to prepare for my burial. Truly I tell you, wherever the gospel is preached throughout the world, what she has done will also be told, in memory of her."* Ask God to create in you a pure heart as Mary demonstrated when she subjected herself to the criticism of others in order to worship Jesus. Ask the Lord to create in you a desire to please him above all else. Then pray for a heart characterized by humility, compassion, and a genuine love for others.

Chapter 20

The Humble are Self-Sacrificial Givers

Jesus sat down opposite the place where the offerings were put and watched the crowd putting their money into the temple treasury. Many rich people threw in large amounts. But a poor widow came and put in two very small copper coins, worth only a few cents.

Calling his disciples to him, Jesus said, "Truly I tell you, this poor widow has put more into the treasury than all the others. They all gave out of their wealth; but she, out of her poverty, put in everything—all she had to live on."

Mark 12:41–44

One of the most interesting statements Jesus makes in this story begins with his words, "Truly I tell you." Throughout the New Testament whenever Jesus wanted to impress a special point on his listeners, he opened with these four words: "Truly I tell you." Jesus punctuated his statement with this authoritative beginning to whatever he was teaching when he wanted to emphasize a specific principle. Here, Jesus says these words as he watches the poor widow put in her two small coins (mites) into the offering receptacle in the court of women. He and his disciples were in the temple observing the rich people throwing in large amounts (out of their great excess and wealth) while the poor widow gave all she had to live on.

This poor widow exemplified being humbly self-sacrificial as she gave away all the money she had. This verse implies she would have nothing left to buy food until she earned more money, thus Jesus' commendation of her steadfast faith and her humble sacrifice. We can imagine Jesus and his disciples sitting there opposite of where people from all walks of life went to contribute their offerings. The rich, as Jesus said, threw in large amounts yet he did not commend any of them for he knew their hearts and he knew their wealth. No matter how much money they gave away, it was out of their abundance. Their giving, though it was a large amount, was not sacrificial. These rich wouldn't have to do without after they gave.

Contrast their giving with the poor widow's, who would most definitely feel the pain of loss. Perhaps she didn't have much, if anything, left at home to eat. Perhaps she went without oil for her lamp. Maybe she had to forfeit fuel for warmth, or possibly even medicine for an illness. Although we don't know the details, the principle is plain. Jesus once again teaches his disciples that it's the attitude of their heart that matters most. Acts of supposed generosity and giving can be good indeed, but to truly demonstrate humility of heart in giving, it must be self-sacrificial.

This story, however, teaches us more than simple guidelines for giving away our material wealth. It similarly implies that in order to give in such a sacrificial way, this poor widow exercised a robust faith, confident that God would provide for her needs. She was compelled by her great love for God to give away all she had to live on. So, when Jesus says "Truly I tell you," he's emphasizing that sacrificial giving in this way pleases God, whether it's in the form of material goods or our time, talents, and energy.

The humble in heart are willingly and joyfully self-sacrificial in every way possible.

✳ ✳ ✳

After studying this passage from Mark's Gospel, we can't help but be moved by the robust faith of this widow who was poor in worldly goods but rich in the abundance of her heart toward God. She lived from one day to the next, very likely not knowing where her next meal would come from, but yet she loved and trusted God to take care of her—even if she gave up all she had to live on. The takeaway from this story isn't a call for us to deplete all our material wealth by giving it away. Rather, it's a lesson in simple faith, humble trust, and a heart fully devoted to God. We see here this poor widow's beautiful act of giving as her outward sign of her worship of God. She gave because she loved God and wanted to honor him with the best she had to give.

So, we must ask ourselves: What is the condition of our hearts? Are we as willing to give our best (material wealth or our time, our talents, and our energy) toward kingdom purposes? Or are we more like the rich who may give more by way of (material wealth) but never give enough to make it sacrificial? Do we part only with our leftovers? Or do we prayerfully give the firstfruits of all we possess to honor God and bless others who are in need?

We would do well to ask ourselves how much we can give rather than how much we can keep for ourselves. When we've been blessed with much, we're in the wonderful position to be generous. Instead of gaining more and more to feed our lusts, our wants, and our desires, we should be excited about how much more we can give away! This isn't to say that we shouldn't be wise savers and planners for future needs. Never that. But we do need to reflect on our true heart attitudes toward all that God has blessed us with in this life. We must be honest with ourselves (and God) daily about how we view these blessings (material wealth and otherwise) as they pertain to our heart. Do we truly love the Creator more than the created blessings he has given us? Today, this very moment, take time to prayerfully reflect on what it might look like for you to give sacrificially.

My Heart's Cry to You, O Lord

Father, help me to grow more sensitive to the many ways I can demonstrate my love for you by becoming a sacrificial giver. You have blessed my life in so many ways. I have been the grateful recipient of your goodness and grace all the days of my life. I want to grow into a more selfless giver, so please open my eyes to the needs of others. Give me opportunities to pass on your generosity to them. Open my eyes. Open my heart. Make me a joyful giver in all ways and in all circumstances. Amen.

The Humble Life in Everyday Life

1. **Humility before God.** *Jesus said, "Truly I tell you, this poor widow has put more into the treasury than all the others. They all gave out of their wealth; but she, out of her poverty, put in everything—all she had to live on."* Pray for God to show you the true condition of your heart as it pertains to giving. Ask him to reveal to you any areas of your life where you hold back from sacrificial giving to him or others. Prayerfully ask God to create in you a thankful, humble, generous spirit that desires to honor him above all else.

2. **Humility before others.** *Jesus said, "Truly I tell you, this poor widow has put more into the treasury than all the others. They all gave out of their wealth; but she, out*

of her poverty, put in everything—all she had to live on."
Look for ways to give your "all" this week to benefit
and bless others. Pray for God to open your eyes to the
needs of others around you and be ready to give sacrificially of your material goods, your time, your talents,
and your energy.

3. **Humility of heart.** *Jesus said, "Truly I tell you, this
   poor widow has put more into the treasury than all the
   others. They all gave out of their wealth; but she, out of
   her poverty, put in everything—all she had to live on."*
   Spend time in prayer this week reflecting on your attitude and choices regarding giving to others. Remind
   yourself that God gives to you so that you can become
   a conduit of blessing to others. Thank him for all the
   blessings and goodness he has bestowed on you as one
   of his beloved children.

Thirty Scripture Verses on Humility

1. The LORD sends poverty and wealth; he humbles and he exalts. (1 Sam. 2:7)

2. "If my people, who are called by my name, will humble themselves and pray and seek my face and turn from their wicked ways, then I will hear from heaven, and I will forgive their sin and will heal their land." (2 Chron. 7:14)

3. You save the humble but bring low those whose eyes are haughty. (Ps. 18:27)

4. He guides the humble in what is right and teaches them his way. (Ps. 25:9)

5. In your majesty ride forth victoriously in the cause of truth, humility and justice; let your right hand achieve awesome deeds. (Ps. 45:4)

6. For the LORD takes delight in his people; he crowns the humble with victory. (Ps. 149:4)

7. He mocks proud mockers but shows favor to the humble and oppressed. (Prov. 3:34)

8. When pride comes, then comes disgrace, but with humility comes wisdom. (Prov. 11:2)

9. Wisdom's instruction is to fear the LORD, and humility comes before honor. (Prov. 15:33)

10. Before a downfall the heart is haughty, but humility comes before honor. (Prov.18:12)

11. He humbles those who dwell on high, he lays the lofty city low; he levels it to the ground and casts it down to dust. (Isa. 26:5)

12. "Has not my hand made all these things, and so they came into being?" declares the LORD. "These are the ones I look on with favor: those who are humble and contrite in spirit, and who tremble at my word." (Isa. 66:2)

13. Seek the LORD, all you humble of the land, you who do what he commands. Seek righteousness, seek humility; perhaps you will be sheltered on the day of the Lord's anger. (Zeph. 2:3)

14. "Take my yoke upon you and learn from me, for I am gentle and humble in heart, and you will find rest for your souls." (Matt. 11:29)

15. "For those who exalt themselves will be humbled, and those who humble themselves will be exalted." (Matt. 23:12)

16. "For all those who exalt themselves will be humbled, and those who humble themselves will be exalted." (Luke 14:11)

17. "I tell you that this man, rather than the other, went home justified before God. For all those who exalt themselves will be humbled, and those who humble themselves will be exalted." (Luke 18:14)

18. "I served the Lord with great humility and with tears and in the midst of severe testing by the plots of my Jewish opponents." (Acts 20:19)

19. By the humility and gentleness of Christ, I appeal to you—I, Paul, who am "timid" when face to face with you, but "bold" toward you when away! (2 Cor. 10:1)

20. Be completely humble and gentle; be patient, bearing with one another in love. (Eph. 4:2)

21. Do nothing out of selfish ambition or vain conceit. Rather, in humility value others above yourselves, not looking to your own interests but each of you to the interests of the others. (Phil. 2:3–4)

22. And being found in appearance as a man, he humbled himself by becoming obedient to death—even death on a cross! (Phil. 2:8)

23. Do not let anyone who delights in false humility and the worship of angels disqualify you. Such a person also goes into great detail about what they have seen; they are puffed up with idle notions by their unspiritual mind. (Col. 2:18)

24. Such regulations indeed have an appearance of wisdom, with their self-imposed worship, their false humility and their harsh treatment of the body, but they lack any value in restraining sensual indulgence. (Col. 2:23)

25. Therefore, as God's chosen people, holy and dearly loved, clothe yourselves with compassion, kindness, humility, gentleness and patience. (Col. 3:12)

26. Who is wise and understanding among you? Let them show it by their good life, by deeds done in the humility that comes from wisdom. (James 3:13)

27. But he gives us more grace. That is why Scripture says: "God opposes the proud but shows favor to the humble." (James 4:6)

28. Humble yourselves before the Lord, and he will lift you up. (James 4:10)

29. In the same way, you who are younger, submit yourselves to your elders. All of you, clothe yourselves with humility toward one another, because, "God opposes the proud but shows favor to the humble." (1 Pet. 5:5)

30. Humble yourselves, therefore, under God's mighty hands, that he may lift you up in due time. (1 Pet. 5:6)